T0122182

THE
HIDDEN RIVIERA

Exploring Southeastern France

Toni Logan and Mal Logan

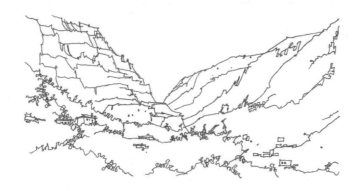

Drawings by Michael Lindell

Order this book online at www.trafford.com
or email orders@trafford.com

Most Trafford titles are also available at major online book retailers.

© Copyright 2009 Toni and Mal Logan.
All rights reserved. No part of this publication may be reproduced, stored in a retrieval
system, or transmitted, in any form or by any means, electronic, mechanical, photocopying,
recording, or otherwise, without the written prior permission of the author.

Book design by Guy Holt
Maps by Guy Holt and Melanie Chipperfield

By the same authors:
Mediterranean Journeys in Time and Place: A Travellers Guide,
Melbourne, 2000

Note for Librarians: A cataloguing record for this book is available from Library
and Archives Canada at www.collectionscanada.ca/amicus/index-e.html

Printed in Victoria, BC, Canada.

ISBN: 978-1-4269-0151-5 (Soft)
ISBN: 978-1-4269-0153-9 (e-book)

*We at Trafford believe that it is the responsibility of us all, as both individuals
and corporations, to make choices that are environmentally and socially sound.
You, in turn, are supporting this responsible conduct each time you purchase a
Trafford book, or make use of our publishing services. To find out how you are
helping, please visit www.trafford.com/responsiblepublishing.html*

*Our mission is to efficiently provide the world's finest, most comprehensive
book publishing service, enabling every author to experience success.
To find out how to publish your book, your way, and have it available
worldwide, visit us online at www.trafford.com*

Trafford rev. 7/21/2009

Front cover: Le Bar-sur-Loup

 www.trafford.com

North America & international
toll-free: 1 888 232 4444 (USA & Canada)
phone: 250 383 6864 ♦ fax: 250 383 6804 ♦ email: info@trafford.com

Acknowledgements

Various people have assisted at different times in the production of this book. They carry no responsibility but we would like to thank them: Kate Logan, Richard Feakes, John Button, Joan Grant, Tony Pritchard, Derek Diamond, Amédée Dellepiane, Leo and Anne West, Loretta Doran, Michael Nelson, Rauni Fertin, Jean-Louis Croquet, the people of Le Bar-sur-Loup, and especially John Evans.

To the memory of John Button–who climbed the highest mountains.

Contents

FOREWORD

Flying into Nice airport on a cloudless day is a unique experience. From the air the *Côte d'Azur* immediately lives up to expectations: a shimmering sea, the beautiful Bay of Angels with its uniformly high apartment blocks along the *Promenade des Anglais,* pockets of glamorous wealth at Cap Ferrat, Villefranche and Monaco, and the *Grande Corniche* whose spectacular views stretch from Old Nice to Menton. A closer look, though, reveals how confined all this is to a narrow coastal belt. Suddenly and sharply behind it are mountains, range after range of rugged landforms, mostly unoccupied and somewhat mysterious.

People who live along the coast enjoy it but feel there are too many tourists, too much congestion and too much crime. On the other hand they speak of the mountains with a kind of reverence and are fascinated by their wild beauty, the deep gorges and the small perched villages. They make frequent journeys there to buy cheeses, honey and fiery liqueurs, to collect mushrooms, to follow walking trails and to lunch at one of the small *auberges.* Yet these highlands that abound in spectacular landscapes and turbulent histories are little known and rarely visited by tourists, either from France or other countries.

Despite isolation and rugged terrain the Maritime Alps have been one of the most fought-over parts of France. Great generals and their armies have struggled through them: Hannibal and his elephants, Caesar and the Roman legions, Napoleon on his march back from Elba and the Allied and German armies in the twentieth century. This is where Vauban built his finest forts to defend French territory against frequent invasions by the Dukes of Savoy in the seventeenth century. And some of the most violent religious wars between the Cathars, the Huguenots and the established Church were fought here. But the story is not all about wars; this alpine area was an important channel for enlightened ideas from the Romans to the Renaissance, some of them now represented in the art and architecture of small isolated villages and tiny chapels.

To newcomers like us and to most visitors, the Riviera coast is easy to understand but the mountains beyond are a challenge. From our base in the village of Le Bar-sur-Loup, only 20 kilometers from Nice and Cannes, we made many journeys into this hidden corner of France. Each became something of a voyage of discovery of little known landscapes, people and places touched by history. What follows is an account of some of these journeys, presented not as ends in themselves but in the hope that they will motivate others to seek out their own parts of unknown rural France.

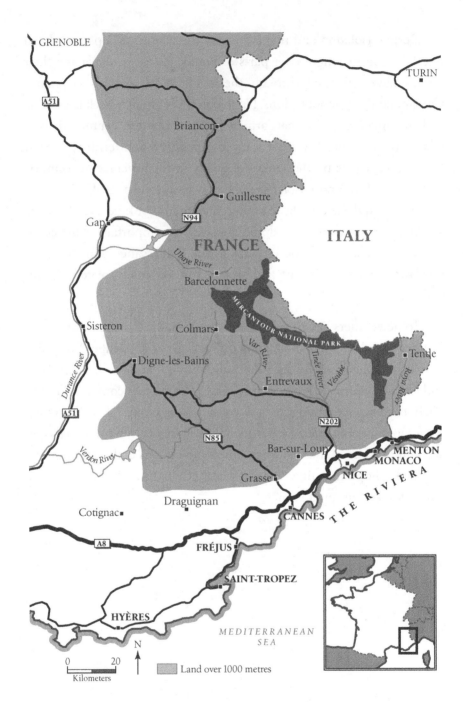

SOUTHEASTERN FRANCE

Chapter One

LIVING THERE

We first came to the Loup Valley by accident. Our explorations of the French countryside had begun many years before when we grew to love the varied landscapes ranging from dark forests, vineyards and wheat fields in the north to the bright, spindly woodlands, olive terraces and hilltop villages in the south. There were, however, particular attractions that brought us to the southeastern corner: striking limestone gorges and mountains, mild winters, the absence of strong mistral winds that dominate other parts of Provence; as well as proximity to cosmopolitan cities and an international airport.

A friend had recommended the hamlet of Pont-du-Loup as a good place for a holiday. It turned out to be a great location beside the tiny Loup River and its impressive gorge where water gushes through whirlpools and over small waterfalls. Even in the dry summer the thickly wooded ravine is cool and humid. Our stay confirmed this was a particularly beautiful part of France hidden away from the noise, bustle and sometimes ugly development of the Riviera. In addition, access from Nice airport was easy, involving only ten minutes along the busy A8 autoroute before branching off to quiet roads leading through pleasant villages to Grasse, the Pre-Alps and the Loup Valley. Daily life in the small villages was relaxed and tranquil - an ideal location for a holiday home.

LOUP VALLEY ENVIRONS

So we decided to buy a house where we could spend long European summers. We knew already that we didn't want to live on the coast despite the images of warmth and luxury. For centuries people from northern Europe and the United States have been coming in their thousands to the coastal strip from St Tropez to Menton, where between June and September tourists are everywhere: prices are high, traffic congestion is awful, crime rates are disturbing and local people less helpful. The *Côte d'Azur* has to a large extent been spoiled by its own attractions.

With the aid of a few agents we confined our search to the villages of the *arrière pays*, the so-called 'back country' which for the most part looks northward to the great mountains. Our requirements were simple: the house should be within a one-hour drive of the airport, outside a village yet easily accessible to its services, have two bathrooms and a bushy garden. And we did not want a ruin that had to be 'done up.'

After only a week of searching we settled on a place just outside the village of Le Bar-sur-Loup. Its immediate attractions were a large *jardin sauvage*, or wild garden, and views toward the perched village of Gourdon, the Loup Gorge and row after row of enticing mountains. Built fairly recently in simple Provencal style the house sits on terraced slopes that until post-war times were part of a commercial olive farm; ten of the old olive trees have survived. In the wild garden citrus fruit prosper, as well as a variety of cool climate fruits such as cherries and walnuts and drought-resistant flowers like agapanthus and oleander - even roses flourish.

Our first stay at the house was in mid-winter when we set about enjoying the weather: the days were golden, the nights cold and there was snow on the nearby hills. A major problem then surfaced. Suddenly the central heating system, *le chauffage*, stopped working. The previous owner had left a list of workmen so we contacted the one for heating and eventually a man appeared, fiddled with the oil pipe to the furnace, got it going but it went out soon after he left - a process repeated several times. Exasperation, even desperation, began to descend and as a last resort we asked for help, in broken French, from the friendly plumber who had come to fix a leaking pipe. Somewhat uncertainly he agreed to have a look at the furnace and after some 'experimentation' he eventually fixed it. We promptly celebrated with a bottle of red; the beginning of a friendship that has served us well. As our problems multiplied his expertise has expanded from plumbing to include heating, swimming pool maintenance, electrical repairs and gardening; and he has kept an eye on the place during our absences.

As apartment dwellers with a terrace of potplants at home, we have had to come to terms with our *jardin sauvage*. Several trees were dying – notably tragic was the huge old walnut tree that shaded the main bedroom in summer. We tried all the recommended remedies but over the years it produced a pale smattering of foliage and many dead branches. Much to the dismay of our squirrels, it had to go.

The mild rainy winters following hot dry summers encourage rapid growth requiring frequent pruning of trees, vines and shrubs. Locals insist that olive trees should be cut back fiercely every second year to improve the olive yield in quantity and size of fruit, but when our olives were made into oil at the nearby mill, the flavor was inferior to that from professional farms nearby so we have kept our ancient olive trees in almost pristine condition. At the end of spring we have a carpet of tiny white flowers followed in early winter by undersized fruit, but the subtle grey-green silvery foliage increases over time.

Since those early days we have come to know and enjoy Le Bar-sur-Loup. There are many pleasures in the warm, cloudless days and long summer twilights, yet life can be exasperating. The lovely fireflies of June give way to stinging insects that can make living outside less pleasant. There are also difficulties in getting things done: a simple problem can suddenly require a much more complex solution than imagined; what one might expect to do in half an hour can take half a day. But this is what it is like and you either take it or leave it. As we now understand the character of the place, what seem at the time to be insurmountable problems eventually fade away in the context of a more leisurely way of life.

—⁂—

Many centuries ago Ligurians and Celts settled around here. Later the ancient Greeks established ports at Marseilles, Antibes and Nice but did not venture inland. It was the Romans who lingered, constructing solid buildings, some of whose foundations have been found beneath the *donjon* in the main square of the village. The word Bar is of Latin derivation indicating the existence of a substantial Roman camp, known as *Castrum Albarnum*. No doubt the abundant water supply from a mountain spring was critical in choosing this location and water from this spring still flows in the *Place de la Fontaine*. As well, a defensive hillside location enabled the Romans to warn neighbouring villages of imminent invasions. Latin inscriptions such as the one embedded at the foot of the bell tower suggest that the period of Roman settlement lasted more than a century.

The medieval period was important. The mild climate and fertile soils of the Loup Valley encouraged intensive farming of grains and vegetables with olives and fruit on the slopes. Higher up, sheep and goats scrambled over the limestone rocks and mules were the beasts of burden. This was also the time when the physical structure of the village – its configuration of streets and buildings – set the pattern for much of what remains today, although many buildings were altered

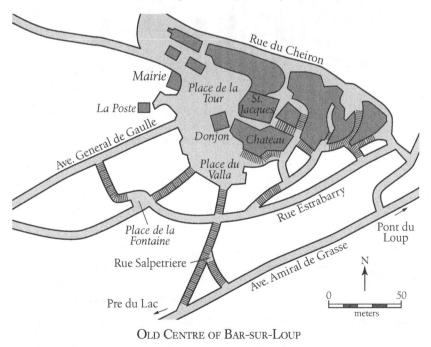

OLD CENTRE OF BAR-SUR-LOUP

during restoration after earthquakes.

Two buildings stand out: the church in mainly Romanesque style and the remains of a chateau, both sitting at the top of the old village beside the *Place de la Tour*. Built between the twelfth and fifteenth centuries, the church is dedicated to the apostle James (St Jacques le Majeur) whose body, some believe, was taken to Compostella de Santiago, the end point of the famous pilgrim's route through southern France and Spain. The church contains several treasures: a renowned altarpiece attributed

LA FONTAINE

to one of the Nice School of artists, and a fascinating painting, the *Danse Macabre*, hung in semi-darkness at the rear. A medieval relic of considerable importance it is said to depict the brutal punishment handed out to anyone attending a ball given by the Count of Bar during the period of Lent.

Little is left of the old chateau. Apparently the original building, a sturdy defense fortress, dates from the tenth century but many additions were made including three round corner towers. It was once connected to the church by a secret passageway, now sealed off, running down the hillside under the houses to the valley far below. The building was damaged by revolutionary forces in 1790 and an earthquake in 1887. The remaining *donjon* now houses the tourist office. A few meters away a section of the chateau has recently been converted into a luxury

ST. JACQUES CHURCH

restaurant and hotel.

The chateau's main claim to fame, though, is that it was home to the Counts of Grasse. One family member, the *Admiral de Grasse*, whose imposing statue stands in front of the church, played a vital role in the United States War of Independence by helping to defeat the English navy at the Battle of Yorktown in 1781. Each year, at the end of September, French and American marines gather in the *Place de la Tour* to celebrate the admiral's victory; the French love such occasions and this one is quite stirring when the bands strike up the *Star Spangled Banner* and the *Marseillaise*.

Ramparts were built around this small central square in the ninth century; houses of three and four storeys were tightly packed into the walls and are now prized residences because of their outlook over the gorge. Many dwellings have wooden beams, little balconies and a lintel engraved with the date of construction. Old timber doors have beautiful knockers made from metal, often in the shape of hands complete with rings and a sleeve cuff. As in most medieval villages the parking of

LE DONJON

cars is one issue always likely to cause a confrontation. Houses in the narrow, winding streets have no off-street parking but there is always an expectation that there will be space for a car, *sans payant*, somewhere nearby. A few small shops and offices are strung out along the main street, with the not unusual name of *Avenue du Général de Gaulle*, that links the *Route Principale* to the *Place de la Tour*. There is a tiny but surprisingly adequate supermarket, a baker, pharmacy, two doctors, a dentist, a butcher and a tabac for newspapers and cigarettes. In later times the post office, *la Poste*, and the town hall, *la Mairie*, have been added in quite imposing buildings.

When the nearby town of Grasse developed a major perfume industry Le Bar-sur-Loup prospered because it contributed a vital ingredient: essence from the blossoms of bitter oranges, the *bigarade*.

A large perfume factory employing more than 800 workers now exists just outside the village; although orange essence is no longer required, production has diversified into artificial flavors and aromas. Nevertheless the village celebrates its tradition as the 'City of Oranges' in an annual festival on Easter Monday when home-made *vin d'orange* is consumed

in large quantities. Also nearby a successful government-sponsored science city, Sophia Antipolis, has brought high-tech enterprises from around the world. And many people from the congested coastal strip have come to live permanently in this back country, as have lots of expatriate Europeans.

Paragliding is a relatively new activity: the clear skies, cliffs and coastal breezes are ideal. Flyers backpack their heavy gear to a plateau edged by a steep scarp near Gourdon. Having climbed into the cumbersome machine the paraglider takes a short run toward the precipice when the wind gusts are just right and takes off like a giant eagle, soaring effortlessly above valleys, villages and sea. A small group of champion gliders has settled around Le Bar and established a business designing and producing the flying machines.

Economic growth and population diversity, then, have vitalised this village of 2,500 people. It is far removed from the postcard prettiness of many French settlements and remains a working village but one where pride in the place is obvious. Its houses have been carefully restored and are well-kept. A lot of public money is spent on cleaning streets, planting gardens, pruning trees and maintaining the cheerful little cemetery. World War II was tough here and the village reminds us of this with a few simple plaques on houses and roadsides mentioning those who died there 'for the glory of France'.

———⌒∿∿⌒———

Around Le Bar there is the usual range of supermarkets but it is in the smaller specialized shops and regular open air markets where customers are really challenged by the local produce: goat cheeses, mountain honey, courgette flowers, fresh herbs, olives, and terrines. If luxury goods are needed, only fifteen minutes away is the old town of Valbonne where wealthy holiday-makers congregate and English is widely spoken, but for high quality *anything* Cannes and Nice are just down the road.

While decisions about food and drink are serious, shopping is also a social occasion. Customers not only greet each other but invariably exchange niceties with the shop-owners, a procedure that can be both pleasing and exasperating. Waiting in the queue can take a long time because each customer is treated as if no one else is there while the pros and cons of each item are thoroughly canvassed as is any family or local news. Finally there is a collective, silent sigh of relief as the customer counts out the notes and low value tiny coins, usually from different pockets in a wallet. *C'est comme ca* – take it or leave it.

Often in a French village one particular shopkeeper becomes known as a 'character' *(un original)* who is the chief conduit and generator of local information and gossip. In Le Bar for many years the butcher played this role; he was more widely known for his extra friendly personality than for the quality of his meat. As newcomers to his crowded little shop he, who spoke no English, learned who we were, told us that his next door neighbour had an Australian son-in-law,

RUE SALPETRIERE

helped us with French grammar and dashed off a sketch of an Akubra hat with 58 written beside it. The following year he rejoiced in the hat and we in free terrines.

We interact daily with the *librairie/tabac*, a tiny shop crammed with newspapers, books and cigarettes, usually sold by the carton. To begin with our conversations were stilted but after a couple of years goodwill was firmly established when we explained that we were being undercharged for our English newspaper. This assertion caused disbelief, followed by consternation and a lengthy discussion involving the four other customers in the shop. When the matter was resolved we became heroes, a status that was enhanced when they learned we were not *en passage* but actually owned a property nearby. Each year now there are fond farewells as we leave and a warm welcome when we return.

A small family bakery operates in the heart of the village. The son bakes bread of 'rural authenticity' in an ancient oven and his elderly mother handles the sales. One Sunday morning we found ourselves in another long queue to buy not just some bread but two bottles of interesting wine on shelf display as well. The latter caused great confusion as the elderly one wildly punched prices into the cash register. Eventually the queue became involved and sorted out not only the price of the wine but how to use a cash register. An air of benign tolerance descended as one customer explained 'people only buy bread here'.

Among the restaurants *La Jarrerie* in its old monastery is widely respected for high quality cuisine, yet our favorite is the *Auberge des Gorges du Loup* in Pont-du-Loup, ten minutes away. Here Monsieur and Madame Blavette have converted an old inn into a modest but charming restaurant with rooms. Located at the entrance to the gorge, it confronts a golden limestone cliff face; dining beneath the palm trees on warm summer evenings or in front of an open fire in winter is something to look forward to.

The French public health system is one of the world's best and is certainly used intensively. A visit to the local doctor is quite an experience. Appointments are rarely made so waiting rooms are almost full. Each arrival greets other patients in a surprisingly jovial manner and the hub of conversation is about life in general as well as illnesses. No private space here! All this is repeated in the pharmacy downstairs. In fact, a formal welcoming of all-comers through language, eye contact and a general air of bonhomie is characteristic of most social situations in the south.

—⁓⁓—

In the following chapters we travel further afield, describing journeys from our base at Bar-sur-Loup to lesser-known parts of southeastern France. Many of these excursions can be covered easily in a day, others may take a week. Generally the large towns are avoided and D roads are recommended: although sometimes narrow and winding they are usually in excellent condition. Given the large amount of information about accommodation in Michelin and other guides, and on the Internet, we mention only those hotels and restaurants where we have been pleasantly surprised.

Overall, the medieval perched villages proved to be the most compelling attractions but it was impossible to ignore the striking natural landscapes: jagged mountains and deep gorges. As well, we were drawn to the ancient rock engravings around Mount Bego, the pilgrimage routes into the highlands and the tracks taken by Hannibal and Napoleon. Many of these journeys took us into virtually uncharted territory; and the hope of discovering more brings us back each year-- even if it means travelling half way round the world just to be there.

PERCHED VILLAGES

Chapter Two

PERCHED VILLAGES:
THE GREAT SURVIVORS

For thousands of years perched villages have been the pre-eminent form of rural settlement in the highlands of southeastern France. There are literally dozens of them, more than in any other part of the country. Clinging to hilltops or hillsides, defense played a key role in determining their location: commanding views over the countryside could warn of marauding tribes and invading armies. Later, they were refuges from plagues and from violent religious and political unrest.

Some perched villages are quite close to the Mediterranean: Mougins, for example, is only four kilometers from Cannes. Others, like Gourdon, have a balcony view to the sea. Many overlook river valleys as their name frequently indicates; thus Le Bar-sur-Loup and Tourrettes-sur-Loup. Closer to the Alps, among the gorges and craggy mountains, these tiny settlements are truly isolated. Yet despite their location all are seductive even when, as in Grasse and Vence, they have been overtaken by urban growth so that now each is the center of a large town.

Seen from afar the key elements of village structure are easily discernible. The sturdy stone walls often consist of tightly packed houses. The Romanesque church has a belfry whose strong vertical lines contrast sharply with softer rural landscapes. There may also be a small chateau, once occupied by a seigneurial family and not destroyed by the revolutionary ardour of the 1790s.

Inside the ramparts, perhaps through an ancient covered gateway, the paved streets are narrow and winding, often crossed by steps so that driving and parking a car can be almost impossible. Usually the houses are small with a large doorway providing access to olive vats, grape presses and a tiny courtyard. Traditionally the family lived on the next level in dark, shuttered rooms while in the attic grain was stored and, occasionally, silkworms reared. These stone buildings, shaded alleys and substantial walls generate an overpowering sense of medieval times. Dotted throughout the village are a few shady squares, one where the men play bowls in late afternoons and another set aside for the weekly market. Old street fountains still bring water from mountain springs for drinking and washing: reminders of the significance of communal life in these isolated villages.

—◈—

It seems that many perched villages were built initially by the Ligurians, people who moved into Provence from northwestern Italy around 1000 BC. They grazed sheep and goats and sought secure sites to protect their animals from thieving neighbors. These earliest villages probably comprised rough wooden huts grouped within a simple wooden fence into which the herds were driven each night. Around 600 BC the Greeks came to the western coast of Provence not as conquerors but as traders searching for supplies of salt. Legend has it that a Ligurian chief's daughter chose the captain of the Greek fleet as her future husband and that her dowry included the land on which Marseilles stands. Several other trading posts were established including Nice and Antibes but the Greeks did not venture into the interior yet the vine and olive plants they introduced were quickly adopted there.

The Romans began arriving about 100 BC bringing impressive engineering skills that allowed them to build an extensive network of paved roads, long-distance aqueducts and huge amphitheaters. Many villages were fortified to serve as key defense posts: ramparts were strengthened; wells were dug to ensure a steady water supply and better access roads built. Because of their height the hilltop villages were vital to the optical communication system introduced by the Romans whereby messages were sent by beacon, smoke and flashes of light on metal, all much faster than a horse-rider. Eventually this system stretched from Rome to the English Channel.

But the Roman genius lay more in its ability to sustain a long period free from internal disorder and external invasion. This *Paix Romaine* lasted for about three centuries during which the improved infrastructure and the system of law and order led to increased productivity in agriculture and to expanded trade. The coastal areas boomed, attracting people away from their villages, some of which were left deserted. Soon after the Romans left though, a series of barbarian tribes moved into the region. Those with the greatest impact, Saracens, were a diverse group of Muslims from North Africa and Southern Spain who became notorious pirates, plundering trading ships and coastal settlements. From their base near the site of modern St Tropez they moved inland; at Gourdon, for example, the remains of a Saracen fortress lie beneath the existing chateau. Local people retreated into the highlands and to those villages that had been fortified by the Romans.

At much the same time a more horrific invasion struck southeastern France - the bubonic plague arrived. Carried by the black rat flea, this outbreak originated in East Africa, traveled north along the Nile to the great port of Alexandria where the rats feasted on the grain stored in ships destined for Mediterranean ports. Ancient records tell of horrendous symptoms: internal hemorrhages, massive pain and insanity. While physicians practised blood-letting, applied magical armlets and opium, townspeople huddled together in their houses or escaped to the hill towns. Many other plagues followed: in the 1340s it was the Black Death that covered the skin with black blotches and in the 1720s the Great Plague resulted in hundreds of bodies piled on the streets of Marseilles.

—◁◁◁▷▷▷—

As if barbarians and plagues were not enough, in the Middle Ages much of Mediterranean France was rent by religious passions that spilled over into the villages. Cathars, for example, wanted a simple religion, away from the ostentation and formalities associated with popes and bishops, but these beliefs were regarded as heretical and led to violent confrontations. In the towns penitents in their hooded cloaks paraded the streets persuading sinners to seek forgiveness and help the poor. Initially supported by the church hierarchy these fraternities came to be regarded as a threat and were forced to disband although a few survived until the twentieth century. Even today at the entrance to many villages one finds a small chapel of the White, Black or Grey Penitents; good examples are at La Tour, Magagnosc and Tende.

Peasants in the isolated northern valleys began to build their own tiny chapels sometimes in the village but quite often along the wayside. Romanesque in style they had a simple rectangular floor plan, small windows, austere facades and a distinctive square belfry. Seeking divine protection from wars and plauges, the peasants, being illiterate, decorated the interior walls with frescoes illustrating the life of Jesus, frequently painted by itinerant Italian artists of the Nice School of painting. With their austere exterior hiding a rich and colorful interior many chapels are now seen as guardians of medieval religious art. Good examples are St Sébastien at Venanson, St Antoine at Clans and, perhaps the best of the lot, Notre-Dame-des Fontaines at La Brigue.

The idea of reforming the Catholic Church gained increasing support: French Protestants, the Huguenots, established their own Reform Church and some hilltop villages in the southeast (like Le Broc) became entirely Protestant and others (like Vence) were overwhelmingly Catholic. Passionate hatreds culminated in the Wars of Religion during which thousands of Huguenots were killed; others migrated to more tolerant nations. Throughout these troubled times perched villages remained a stronghold for dissenters.

By the eighteenth century France was in a state of political unrest. Peasants had suffered a series of disasters: severe frosts killed many olive trees, silk harvests were poor and wine prices were falling. The Jacobins, a radical political group, advocated an egalitarian democracy and struggled to reduce the high taxation that had financed royal extravagances. The 1789 Revolution brought matters to a head. Extremists gained control and established a republic that condoned the destruction of feudal chateaux and the pillage of church properties. In the reign of terror that followed, countless royalists were sent to the guillotine and anarchy took over. In the southeast support was bitterly divided between republican and royalist factions sometimes leading to bloody conflicts between neighboring villages.

But economic conditions changed: manufacturing industries expanded, agriculture became more mechanized and transport was vastly improved. Southeastern France, however, had very few resources with which to participate in this industrial growth and much of the region had fallen on bad times. What is now the *Côte d'Azur* was little more than a collection of small fishing ports whose sole redeeming feature was the mild Mediterranean winter. As the coast became more accessible by railway and highway, wealthy people from cold northern Europe were drawn to the Riviera's hotels and casinos, to the palm-lined promenades and to its manicured beaches, all of which generated jobs and income for the local inhabitants.

Nevertheless the future of the *arrière pays* still looked bleak. Rural to urban migration accelerated as more and more villagers abandoned their picturesque surroundings to participate in the nearby prosperity. Yet, as so often in the past, circumstances changed. What had begun as a trickle of aristocratic visitors in the sunny winters became a flood of summer tourists. The impact of this tourist boom on the villages was selective: many experienced a new burst of life while retaining their medieval character, some became commuter suburbs to the large coastal towns yet others provided holiday homes. On the other hand a few became derelict, even deserted. Despite these differences, travelling through the area today one cannot fail to be impressed with its overall vitality and prosperity. It is possible to visit many lively perched villages in short trips from Nice. In particular we recommend Gourdon, St Paul de Vence and Vence itself. Each has a medieval centre as well as a major feature of contemporary art.

Gourdon is quite special: a breathtaking location, a well-preserved chateau, famous gardens and deservedly classified as one of the *Plus Beaux Villages de France*. Towering some 500 meters above the Loup Gorge, seen at night from Le Bar the village resembles a cluster of bright stars but during the day it is more like an eagle's nest. As the Romans and Saracens recognized, the site was ideal for keeping watch over the coastal plain. The path up to the village from Pont-du-Loup climbs an almost sheer cliff that redoubtable traders must have negotiated with heavily-laden mules. This Saracen track remains as a signposted walk called the *Chemin du Paradis* – not because it reaches toward heaven but from the Provencal word *paradou*, meaning near water. A short walk from the car park leads to a splendid panorama from *Place Victoria*. Many of the old houses have been converted into shops selling locally made scents, soap, fruit wines, candles and glass; and of the few restaurants we recommend *La Taverne Provencale* for its good food, spectacular views and cool breezes on hot nights.

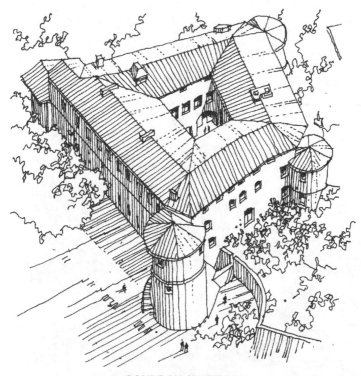

GOURDON CHATEAU

Since the ninth century the small Saracen fortress and chateau have been re-built: rounded corner towers, steep walls and a dungeon were added. The castle was then substantially redesigned into its current form - a trapezium surrounding an arcaded courtyard. Very recently it became home to the *Musée des Artes Décoratifs et de la Modernitée*, exhibiting a superb display of Art Deco furniture. The basic design of the gardens is attributed to the renowned French landscape architect, André le Nôtre, whose major work had been the grand vistas and ornamental lakes at Versailles. Clearly the Gourdon site could not accommodate such an ambitious plan. Instead le Nôtre proposed small formal gardens planted with box and yew trees to be clipped into spheres and cones arranged in linear patterns. Guided tours through the castle and its gardens are

CHATEAU GARDENS

particularly worthwhile.

St Paul, proudly silhouetted on a hill just down the road from Vence, is a showpiece medieval village augmented by an outstanding collection of contemporary art. Little is known about the Roman origins of St Paul but its primary function was to guard against attacks from the neighboring state of Savoy. The massive walls, still intact, were not built until the sixteenth century when Francois I decided to turn the town into a strategic fortress as a part of his grand plan to defend the entire Var Valley. Constructing the ramparts was a huge task necessitating the demolition of 700 houses whose inhabitants were moved to the nearby town of La Colle. A walk around the ramparts provides great views in all directions.

The main entrance is through a tunneled archway – the *Porte de France* – leading to the narrow cobbled *Rue Grande* with its bright shops, lively cafés, flower-decked balconies and artists' studios. St Paul and Tourrettes may appear somewhat like museums in their artistic and tourist characters but they do retain the essential features of the perched village. The Gothic church is rich in works of art with two especially fine pieces by Tintoretto and Murillo.

In common with many villages, religion played an important role in the story of St. Paul; in fact its dominance probably persisted longer here than elsewhere. It began in 1665 when the Bishop of Grasse founded the Order of the White Penitents. Dressed in their white hoods and cloaks the Penitents regularly paraded though the village in a long procession to celebrate the Lord's Supper in the *Chapelle Saint-Croix*. They also processed in large numbers at night holding candles and looking like ghosts – a ceremony that continued until 1918.

But St Paul went into decline while nearby Vence flourished and it was not until the 1920s that it sprang into life again. This was when Paul Roux the owner of a small café, the *Colombe d'Or*, became so concerned about the welfare of artists who had migrated from the coast that he accepted their paintings as payment for their meals. Over the years the small café has become an expensive *auberge* and home to a wonderful collection by world famous artists including Renoir, Utrillo, Matisse, Vlaminck, Picasso and Bonnard. To view these works the price is an expensive meal or an overnight stay.

FONDATION MAEGHT

St Paul is also home to the *Fondation Maeght*, one of Europe's finest museums of contemporary art. It is funded entirely by Marguerite and Aimé Maeght, whose Catalan architect, Jose Luis Sert, designed a cluster of buildings and a sculpture garden: a quite unique blend of indoor and outdoor spaces that fit perfectly with the local environment. Sert collaborated with other artists including his compatriot Miro whose ceramics, mosaics and fountains immediately welcome the visitor. Braque decorated a pool and the stained glass windows in the tiny chapel. The permanent collection contains outstanding works by Kandinsky, Bonnard, Chagall and Giacometti; outside, the landscaped gardens have sculptures by Calder, Miro and many others. Rather expensive to enter the *Fondation Maeght* is worth every cent.

Perched on a south-facing hillside, Vence has a very long history. About ten kilometers from the sea, with lots of sun, sheltered from the winter winds, and overlooking the Mediterranean this was a great place for a town. Originally the capital of the Ligurians it became an important Roman military base with road connections to other parts of the empire and was also the nerve-center for the visual communication network of nearby perched villages. Attacked by the Lombards and then the Saracens it was later to join the front line of wars between France and Savoy. When it became the episcopal center of the bishops Vence expanded its regional influence but did not escape the turbulent conflict between the Church and the Villeneuve family that extended until the end of the Wars of Religion in the sixteenth century.

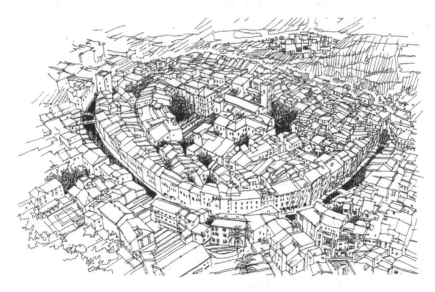

VENCE

In the early Middle Ages the Villeneuves established themselves as lords of Vence. Like the Grimaldis of Cagnes and the Lascaris from Tende they controlled an area stretching to the Italian border. Operating outside the control of the king these feudal lords made life insecure, especially for those in villages along the frontier. The founder of the dynasty, *Romée de Villeneuve*, is renowned for the innovative way he solved the town's financial crisis: he married each of his four daughters into royalty, one becoming Queen of England and another the Empress of Austria.

The lively bustle of present-day Vence is concentrated in the small, elliptical *Vieille Ville*, the original medieval settlement surrounded by fortress walls. The main entrance, *Porte Peyra*, passes under a watchtower once owned by the Villeneuve family and now an important art gallery. Directly ahead in *Place Peyra* is the old Roman forum which later was the site of the Revolutionary guillotine. Now an attractive open-air shopping center in a shady environment with many restaurants it is home to an elegant urn-shaped fountain that until recently drew the town's water supply from *La Foux*, a spring in the limestone rocks to the north. The narrow *Rue du Marché*, running off the square, is the market street, with no souvenirs for tourists, but lots of fruit, fresh foods and flowers for the locals. Despite the large number of tourists, Vence has an air of independent wealth about it, of modern comfortable living in an old world environment.

Given its long history as an episcopal seat, Vence has several chapels which display rich ecclesiastical art, nearly all built by penitent fraternities. While the Chapel of the Black Penitents has been demolished, the colorful dome of the Chapel of the White Penitents can still be seen. The St Elizabeth Chapel has fine frescoes, albeit somewhat faded, painted by an itinerant Turin artist; and St Anne's was built specifically to care for mothers and children.

VENCE: PORTE PEYRA AND FOUNTAIN

All these small buildings are historically interesting but the crowning glory in the city's ecclesiastical narrative must be the small chapel designed by Henri Matisse. It is about a 15 minute walk from the old city heading toward St Jeannet (taking you past the excellent restaurant, *Auberge Les Templiers*). Completed in 1952, it was Matisse's gift to the Dominican nuns who had cared for him during a serious illness. Now ranked of world significance, the building itself is quite simple: white with a blue roof and radiant yellow and green stained glass windows. Inside, stark black lines on white walls represent the Stations of the Cross. He designed every detail – even down to the furniture and the priest's vestments: few religious buildings generate such an atmosphere of absolute serenity. The tiny chapel is open only for a few hours each week when it is often swamped by bus-loads of tourists, so it is important to check times with the local tourist office.

Chapter Three

Grasse: Not Just The Scent

During the summer months hordes of tourists are brought by bus
to Grasse from the *Côte d'Azur* to see the large perfumeries and buy
some of their products at bargain prices. At first sight many visitors are
disappointed with this perfume capital of the world: it certainly does
not display the luxury equivalent to *Chanel No. 5* or *Dior's Poison*. Rather
the dominant impression is of a somewhat shabby hillside town looking
out to the Mediterranean Sea over a sprawl of unattractive twentieth
century industrial and commercial buildings. Gone are the great fields
of flowers that once were vital to perfume production.

This is the paradox of Grasse: an old town with a proud history
of sustained economic growth and political independence neither,
however, immediately apparent in the contemporary urban landscape.
Yet Grasse deserves a closer look. A venerable medieval town, its
existence illustrates the abiding gift of water, its persistent links with
north Italian city-states and an ability to grasp changing economic
conditions.

———

The town sits at the southern edge of a large limestone plateau
in the foothills of the Pre-Alps. The soft rock erodes easily into crags,

LA FOUX

cliffs and canyons and is so porous that water seeps through small cracks to form subterranean drainage patterns. Sometimes the seepage is dammed by impervious rock and the pressurized water has to push its way out through another crack in the limestone, resurging as a mountain spring. This has been nature's gift to Grasse: *La Foux*, or 'the gusher'. Until recently, even in the long dry summers, it provided a never-ending supply of mountain water to the town. Now the piped water from the spring can be seen on the *Boulevard du Jeu de Ballon*, next to the municipal tourist office. Its legacy is most obvious in the many old street fountains that once provided clean water for drinking and in the tiny old reservoir in the *Rue du Font Neuve*.

The built-up area of the town grew downhill from *La Foux* allowing the force of gravity to distribute water to many houses (sometimes even to their third floor), street laundries, leather tanneries and small soap workshops. Underground there remains a virtual labyrinth of pipes and channels that carry the water along. Today for a much larger urban population additional water is brought from dams in the Siagne and Loup Gorges.

Few records exist concerning the origin of Grasse itself. Although archeological evidence indicates that small prehistoric settlements were scattered throughout the region, no Roman relics have been found in the town. When they did arrive in the first century BC the Romans met small warlike groups of native Ligurians who subsisted on the inhospitable inland territory by pasturing sheep and growing wheat. In earlier times, from coastal enclaves, Phoenician and Greek traders had exchanged olives and grapes for hides, soap and rough cloth. What the Romans did establish was a peaceful framework within which the area could be utilized more efficiently: large farms with slave labour produced a surplus of agricultural goods and Roman roads allowed rapid movement of goods, as well as troops, over long distances; the *Via Aurelia*, for example, passed through Provence linking Rome to much of Gaul and Spain.

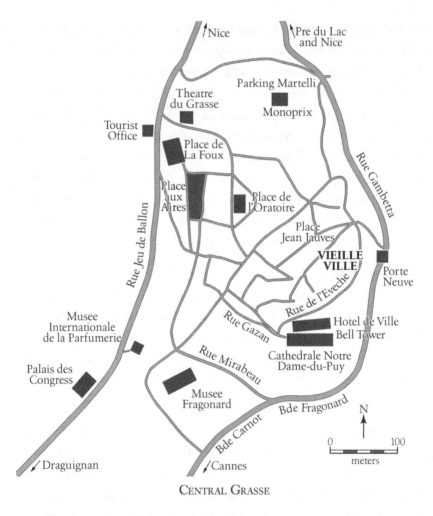

CENTRAL GRASSE

The derivation of the town's name raises interesting questions. Was it honouring Crassus, a Roman general? Or, according to another story, was it to celebrate the grace shown to Jewish refugees who were allowed to settle there in the first century AD? Perhaps this would explain the early skills of the *Grassois* in facilitating trade around the Mediterranean. Yet throughout the Middle Ages there are official references to the town as 'Fatty'!

From the fifth century AD a prolonged series of barbarian invasions contributed to the collapse of the Roman Empire forcing many local inhabitants back to subsistence farming with a little trade on the side. Large ports like Antibes were attacked and often destroyed by the Saracens. Fear of barbarian invasion from the sea meant that the trading frontier moved inland, and the now-fortified town of Grasse, about twenty kilometers from the coast and on a hillside 300 meters above sea-level, possessed the basic elements to operate a warning system and a safe haven when marauding attacks were imminent.

From what one French historian has called 'an acute commercial smell', the *Grassois* were ready and able to seize the opportunity to join the maritime trading network including Genoa, Pisa and Florence. Already the small town had attracted attention for its fine quality leather; during the tanning process local aromatic plants, especially powdered myrtle, were added to make the leather supple and sweet-smelling. Now a wider market sought the product and to meet this demand local entrepreneurs bought untreated hides from Spain and Italy which were then processed for export in return for weapons, silk cloth and luxury items. Less profitable exports included soap, olive oil and woollen cloth. As early as the twelfth century Grasse had become prosperous from the quality of its produce and the business acumen of its traders. In turn, this wealth generated political and physical changes to the town.

The economic power of the merchants in Grasse made it possible to modify the feudal system so that it differed from other parts of France. When the *Grassois* helped defeat the Saracens several warrior chiefs were granted feudal property rights. The locals, though, were not willing to be vassals in service to the *seigneur* but were willing to pay tithes to support the church. So Grasse never fell under the control of such powerful feudal landlords as the Villeneuves of Vence, rather, the property-owning nobility actually became financially and politically weak.

On the other hand the local influential merchant class, drawing on their familiarity with Genoa, in the 12th century adopted a similar style of government: a small, autonomous republic, *Le Consulat de Grasse*. Each year a citizen assembly met to elect four consuls who were to administer a wide jurisdiction including defense, taxation and commerce. The bishop responsible for religious and community affairs in Grasse had fled from Antibes to avoid the Saracens and did not interfere with the consuls' preoccupation with trade. In particular, they sought trading partners with whom they could exchange goods on mutually favorable terms. While the *Consulat* only existed in its republican form for about a hundred years it soon reached this kind of agreement with several Italian cities.

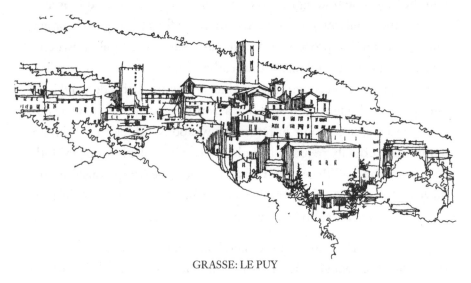

GRASSE: LE PUY

The town's early prosperity can be seen today in the cluster of twelfth century public buildings on *Le Puy*, a relatively high platform of archaic volcanic rock on the southern side of the town. Still standing there is the *Tour de Guet*, easily recognized by its severely pitted surface. Before the town walls were built this primitive fortress, massive and grim, was all that could protect the inhabitants from attack. Later it became part of the bishop's palace and now of the town hall offices, close to an elegant though small, classical garden.

By far the most outstanding structure on the platform is the *Cathédrale Notre-Dame-du-Puy* whose square bell-tower dominates the urban skyline. Although repaired and remodelled many times its simple sober façade of pale limestone is a fine example of Italian Romanesque architecture. It too was fortified as a refuge against enemies such as those who, during a siege in 1589, fired cannons into the facade for seven days. Inside the cathedral the severe style continues: a narrow nave and the high ceiling supported by sturdy columns generate a feeling of enclosure. Benefactors have donated several fine works of art including three paintings by Peter Paul Rubens, a triptych by Louis Bréa and *The Washing of the Feet* by Jean-Honoré Fragonard, a member of the local perfumery family.

Ramparts were built in the twelfth century to encircle these public buildings on tiny *Le Puy* and traces of them can be seen today in *Rue de l'Evéche* beside the *Hôtel de Ville*. During enemy invasions hundreds of farmers would huddle with the townsfolk inside the high walls with all gates securely bolted. The most recent walls were removed only in the nineteenth century but the wide curving boulevards, such as the *Rue Gambetta*, and the new gate, *Porte Neuve*, indicate their location.

The later Middle Ages were a destabilising time for Grasse. Dissension among the ruling families encouraged the Count of Provence to impose his authority over the flourishing commercial center but it appears that the *Grassois* were able to bargain for the retention of some privileges, most importantly the liberty of its citizens. When Provence became part of France in the fifteenth century Grasse was drawn into conflicts about territory and religion; the town was repeatedly attacked, besieged and pillaged by French, Italian, Spanish and Austrian troops. Yet throughout this period the town's industries and trade survived.

Such resilience has been attributed to unusual social structures. The feudal nobility continued to play a relatively unimportant role and many of the manors were acquired by the 'new' nobility: those families whose wealth depended upon commercial and industrial enterprises. Throughout the damaging invasions social classes cooperated to defend the physical and economic infrastructure of the town. Even the political upheavals of the 1789 Revolution and the massive overspending by Napoleon did not break this alliance. Throughout its long history Grasse remained essentially a bourgeois town.

——◦◦◦——

The advent of the leather industry affected the residential areas markedly. At first the tanned leather, soaps and oils were made in people's homes – in the cellar, the attic, even the nearby lanes. Each house was built on a tiny allotment so it could only be enlarged upwards, to five or six storeys. Very few houses remain that pre-date the sixteenth century when the next major upsurge in the town's prosperity occurred, but at No. 11 in the *Place des Soeurs* there is a good example of a fourteenth century merchant's house. The very old town, *la Vieille Ville*, can be identified by the street pattern: tiny, steep winding lanes crossed by flights of steps and archways that resemble trenches or tunnels as the houses shadow the pavements.

Just outside the former town walls is the *Place aux Aires* which was particularly important in the early leather industry. Once a large, breezy area where farmers came to winnow their wheat, the tanners found it an ideal location; not only were the foul smells of their work distanced from the town but a rivulet ran down from *La Foux* providing copious amounts of water to wash the hides and there was space to spread them out to dry. When the leather trade declined the canal was covered and the old buildings refurbished. At the northern end of this rectangular open space is an elegant house at No. 33 that belonged to a merchant and leather tanner. Today the whole area is enclosed by old, narrow, four-storey buildings with small shops and Italianate arcades at ground level. Tall trees shade the open-air cafes that come to life on hot nights when cool breezes blow and dining there can be a pleasant experience with good food at reasonable prices.

After leather came perfume: in the sixteenth century this industrious town became involved in the extremely profitable industry of making scented gloves. Since ancient times flowers, herbs and spices had been used to make scented waters, oils and soaps to reduce the pungent odors of people's homes, their clothes and, most of all, their bodies. With its abundant wild flowers and herbs the town was ideal for producing perfume – early on travelling salesmen mixed potions for individual customers, but later a mass market developed.

PERFUME SELLER CIRCA 1700

In Florence leather clothing – belts, pantaloons and waistcoats – had long been popular. It was even believed that scented gloves gave immunity from plagues; however it was only when a Florentine aristocrat married into the French royal family that this fashion spread. Apparently Catherine de Medici was impressed, not just by Grasse's fine leather but also by the profusion of wild flowers and herbs. She sent for a perfumer experienced in Florentine methods of production to evaluate the potential for the industry's development and his laboratory indicated strong possibilities. So with royal patronage the production of scented gloves took off.

While Grasse had expertise in producing large quantities of leather there was little familiarity with the production of perfume. The oldest method, still used with orange blossom, is distillation whereby vast quantities of petals are boiled to obtain the flower essence which is then condensed in copper vessels up to two meters high. Many of these graceful *alambics* still decorate perfume shops. A second method, used now mainly for jasmine and tuberoses, involves steeping fresh layers of animal fat between layers of flowers and then washing them to separate the perfume from the fat. It takes about 750 kilograms of rose buds to make one kilogram of pure rose essence, a particularly labour-intensive process as the fats must be renewed daily. A third method, used mainly for mimosa, extracts the essence in a concentrated form by using a solvent with the flowers to form a wax which is then removed by alcohol.

ALAMBICS

Financial skills were essential in the town's industrial expansion at this time. Jewish entrepreneurs devised new forms of credit that underpinned a major increase in the export of scented gloves and even enabled local business to invest in a merchant fleet. When the fashion for these gloves declined in the eighteenth century, the specialized manufacture of perfume for its own sake became the major industry. It has continued to expand until now it is one of France's most valuable exports. In Grasse itself the perfume industry is concentrated in three large firms – Galimard, Molinard and Fragonard – all with strong links to Parisian fashion houses and overseas markets. Despite the wealth generated its local impact is not immediately obvious.

Today the chief floral ingredients are jasmine, mimosa, tuberoses and the blossom of bitter orange trees. Some ingredients are only available from overseas: sandalwood from the Solomon Islands, ginger from India and musk from Tibetan deer, for example. Until recently the flower crops were grown on the large plain below Grasse township, now swamped with factories and warehouses, and in the nearby hill country of Plascassier, Bar-sur-Loup and Tourrettes-sur-Loup. Labour requirements were high, especially at harvest time, and as it became much cheaper to import the floral essences very few flower farms now remain.

The early perfume workshops were small and crowded into the old part of the town. Several small establishments still exist, but most visitors head for one of the big three and, of these, Fragonard is closest to the town center. Each firm provides a free tour in English to illustrate modern production methods and to offer a range of perfumed goods. Also very close to the town center, around the *Place du Cours Honoré Cresp*, a group of museums provides insights into the cultural background of perfume, of Grasse and of Provence. The *Musée de la Marine* focuses on the pursuits of the *Admiral de Grasse*; in front is a figure from the seventeenth century painting, *Habit de Parfumeur* often used as a logo in the town.

INTERNATIONAL MUSEUM OF PERFUME

Early in the nineteenth century yet another change occurred in the local economy. For over a millennium Grasse had prospered from the manufacture and trade in leather, soap, oil, cloth, scented gloves and perfume. Now it became a resort for aristocrats from northern Europe seeking sunny winter months. Grasse had much to offer; not simply a pleasant climate but panoramic views, picturesque rural villages and, above all, tranquility. In response to this trend several large hotels and sumptuous villas were built on the northern slopes overlooking the medieval center and with views as far as the Mediterranean.

Three notable women fuelled the town's popularity. Pauline Bonaparte arrived in Grasse in 1807 to recover from family and health problems; a small park in her name recalls daily visits to enjoy the shady olive trees and peaceful views. (In entirely different circumstances her brother was to pass through the town on his escape from Elba in 1815.) Higher up the slope were the extravagantly beautiful gardens of Alice de Rothschild where more than fifty workers cared for hundreds of roses, daisies and tulips and for exotic plants like yuccas, wattle and tropical palms. Eventually the gardens were subdivided for high class residential development so very little remains apart from the difficult-to-find teahouse with its vivid blue and yellow-tiled roof. And in 1891 Queen Victoria and her retinue spent a two-month vacation at the Grand Hotel in *Avenue Thiers*, now a block of apartments that, in faded glory, still looks across to the sea.

In the 1920s, however, the tourist bubble burst: wealthy travelers, especially Americans, preferred summer holidays down on the coast where swimming, sailing and partying became the key attractions. Since then, apart from perfume production, Grasse has been essentially an economic backwater despite the influx of retired people and immigrants from North Africa. It is still the largest town in the back country behind the Riviera and functions as a regional center for education, health and administrative services. Over the past decade efforts have been made to attract visitors for more than just the perfumeries: rationalizing traffic flows in the medieval street pattern, beautifying streets and gardens and promoting cultural festivals. The best way to explore the town is to join a group walking tour organized by the helpful tourist office or to go it alone with a detailed guide map. Parking is a problem but for those wishing to explore the town there is a large undercover car park next to Monoprix in *Place Martelly*.

Of more interest to some visitors perhaps is the splendid restaurant, with rooms, created a decade ago by Jacques Chibois, one of France's best chefs. Located on the western edge of Grasse, *La Bastide Saint-Antoine* is set in spacious grounds that contain an olive grove, gardens and a swimming pool. The 200 year old farmhouse, although converted to modern standards, has retained the ochre colors so typical of Provence and now has three dining rooms as well as a spectacularly-lit terrace with distant views of the Mediterranean. The food is simple, concentrating on local Provencal ingredients but prepared in an innovative way: as for example, ice cream flavored with olives. At the end of a relaxed and reasonably-priced meal, enhanced by low-key friendly service, the overwhelming sensation is of intense flavors that echo the sun-drenched surroundings. M. Chibois' two star Michelin ranking is well deserved.

The countryside near Grasse has many attractions. The limestone caves and gorges near St-Cezaire-sur-Siagne, the feudal castle and Roman wells at Cabris, the tiny fortress village and church square at Auribeau-sur-Siagne and the two surprisingly beautiful churches at Magagnosc are each well worth tracking down. Clearly, to do it justice, the old medieval town of Grasse warrants more than just a day visit to buy perfume.

Chapter Four

Tracking Hannibal and His Elephants

A two-hour drive north from Nice the small alpine basin known as Le Queyras nestles against the Italian border in the high mountains of southeastern France. It was here in 218 BC that the brilliant Carthaginian general, Hannibal Hamilcar, led his huge army over the Alps in a desperate attempt to attack the Romans from the north. This journey and the battles won over the next fifteen years were to make Hannibal the hero of the Punic wars – between Rome and Carthage.

Fought with great ferocity and on a scale unrivalled until the modern era, these Punic Wars lasted for over 100 years but despite Hannibal's many victories, they ended with the Roman capture of Carthage. So deep was their hatred of everything Carthaginian that the Romans annihilated all traces of the once great empire including its buildings, language, writing, culture and religion. They even ploughed salt into the land. Nevertheless, the world remembers Hannibal and the great army of 100,000 infantry, 12,000 cavalry and 37 war elephants that he led from present day Spain up the Rhone Valley and into northern Italy, spurred on by his fierce determination to destroy Rome.

The elephants in particular have captured the imagination of many: large, cumbersome sub-tropical animals struggling over snow-covered mountains. Beyond this image however it is difficult to describe the impact of the elephants in Hannibal's battles because so many historical records were destroyed by the Romans. Yet, from other sources, we do know that war elephants had been used by the Egyptians and Greeks who found they could panic enemy lines; their tough hides would deflect spears and horses were terrified by the noise, smell and size of the large animals and when they carried a 'cage' with up to four soldiers, they were virtually invincible.

There has even been debate about the kind of elephant used by Hannibal. Were they the larger Indian type that was amenable to training yet had to be brought over a long distance or were they from Africa, with shorter distances to travel but more difficult to train for warfare? From a rare Carthaginian coin it seems that they were African, although it has been suggested that Hannibal himself rode a particularly large elephant called Surus – meaning 'from Syria'. So his army possibly included both types.

Who were the Carthaginians? Their civilization originated in Phoenicia at the eastern end of the Mediterranean around the twelfth century BC. From its main city, Tyre, the Phoenicians established trading posts along the coasts of Sicily, Sardinia and, most importantly, North Africa. They never intended these small settlements to become anything more than ports-of-call except for Carthage (near modern Tunis), which grew rapidly because it protected the lucrative silver and iron trade route between Phoenicia and Cadiz in Spain. By the eighth century BC the city became immensely rich and developed its own empire. In its trading activities Carthage learnt to co-exist with the Greeks, but Rome was a different story; by the third century BC it was emerging as a political and military force. Wars with Carthage actually encouraged the consolidation of the Roman Empire which was to dominate much of the known world for the next five centuries.

After its defeat in the First Punic War, Carthage decided to expand its empire in Spain and gave control of the army to Hamilcar Barca whose eldest son, Hannibal, inherited its leadership when he was 26 years old. By that time Spain was a semi-independent part of Carthage and the Barca dynasty had the trappings of a royal family obsessed with avenging the defeat suffered previously at the hands of Rome. Hannibal was convinced that having lost a long war fought at sea the only way now was to attack on land, no easy task as the Roman army occupied the coastal areas along the Mediterranean. So he devised a bold plan to lead his army north through the Rhone Valley and over the Alps to Rome.

HANNIBAL'S ROUTE FROM SPAIN TO ITALY VIA THE ALPS

When he left Spain in the spring of 218 BC with his army of more than 100,000 men, Hannibal knew that speed was of the essence to avoid snow blocking the mountain passes. He knew also that he had to avoid the Roman army that was clustered just south of Arles. The first hurdle, the Pyrenees, was relatively easy but the second, crossing the mighty Rhone, showed how cumbersome elephants could slow down an entire army. Apparently, long rafts were built, lashed together to form a bridge and covered with dirt and grass with the expectation that

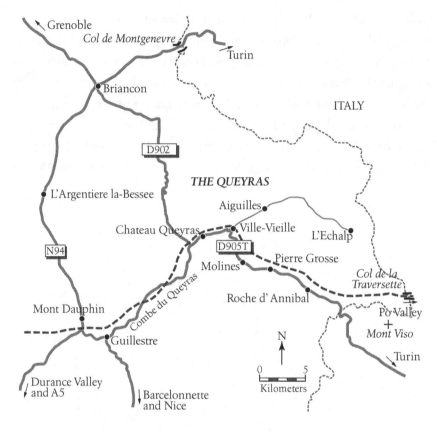

WHERE HANNIBAL CROSSED THE ALPS

the animals would walk on the 'new ground'. When this tactic failed some elephants were shunted into the river and expected to swim but this also failed. Eventually several mature females from the herd were persuaded to walk onto the bridge and the others followed. Having crossed the Rhone, Hannibal turned north and proceeded along the eastern side of the river.

Precisely where he made his next major turn – this time to the east - is debatable, but the only way to the Alps was along one of the transverse valleys cut by the tributaries of the Rhone. By far the most likely route was along the Drôme River, an easy walk that took him into the territory of the Allobroges, a particularly aggressive and devious Gallic tribe. As he moved further east Hannibal became uncertain about the route to follow and was forced to seek guidance from the Allobroges, who despite shows of friendship deliberately misled and ambushed the troops a number of times. Harassment from local tribes continued all the way to the Po Valley in Italy.

Hannibal crossed from the Drôme to the Durance Valley about where Sisteron is today. Once again the walking was easy but he lost his way in the foothills of the Alps. He was guided to what is now the town of Guillestre from where he should have turned left and pressed on to the easy pass at *Col de Montgenèvre*. But he was tricked into entering the deep, narrow gorge cut by the Guil River - the *Combe du Queyras* – as the quickest way across the Alps.

COMBE DU QUEYRAS

Here Hannibal's army suffered the worst ambush. Because of the narrowness of the gorge soldiers could only walk three abreast and elephants in single file so the army was spread over almost the entire eight kilometers length of this deep ravine. The elephants in particular were an easy target for the Gauls who threw spears and rolled down boulders from the ridges above. Many soldiers were killed, others deserted, and the elephants panicked. Having eventually found his way out of the gorge Hannibal was now virtually trapped in Le Queyras. There was certainly no way back and while he could see stretches of level country immediately to the east he could also see the magnitude of the more distant mountains to be crossed. Five months since he left Spain it was now beginning to snow. He had no option but to go straight ahead searching for a pass somewhere north of Mount Viso.

ELEPHANTS IN BATTLE

The most direct route followed a small tributary of the Guil, from the present-day village of Ville Vieille to Molines, where he continued eastward past Pierre Grosse and Fontgillard. Almost directly ahead was the *Col de la Traversette* which, at 3,000 meters is considered to be one of the most difficult passes in the Alps. Yet it is almost certainly the one taken by Hannibal and his men. About one kilometer beyond Fontgillard, a large boulder (identified today as *Rocher D'Annibal* on some maps) on the southern side of the road (D205T) has a plaque indicating that Hannibal passed by it as did Caesar and other more recent heroes of the Alpine country.

It took Hannibal nine days to reach the top of the pass. The climb was extremely difficult for the men but at last they could look across the gathering snow and see the northern plain of Italy. Getting down the mountain slippery with so much ice proved especially difficult for the elephants. It took at least three days to reach the floor of the Po Valley where snow had not yet settled and there was grass for the animals; but the costs had been enormous. Hannibal had probably lost half his original army through deaths and desertions. Those remaining were exhausted but most of the horses and elephants survived, which explains his early success against the Romans. Depleted though it was, his army had made a harrowing journey across virtually unknown territory, something the Romans had believed impossible. One of the boldest ventures in antiquity had come off.

He was to remain in Italy for the next fifteen years fighting and, more often than not, defeating armies in isolated battles, rather than engaging in a massive onslaught on Rome itself. Just why he did not attack Rome when he was probably in a winning position remains a mystery because his military genius was beyond question, as demonstrated in two memorable battles. The first was at Lake Trasimeno where, in 217 BC, he destroyed virtually the entire enemy force of 25, 000. A year later at the small hilltop town of Cannae, although all his elephants were now dead, he won his greatest victory when he annihilated 48,000 of the largest army Rome had ever fielded.

At this famous Battle of Cannae, Hannibal's tactic was to arrange his much smaller army in an unusual convex line facing the enemy, who eagerly charged forward. Slowly the bulge in the Carthaginian line flattened out but only after the enemy infantry had lost their neat formation and most of their energy. Eventually the center gave way, so Hannibal's line was now concave and the Romans, scenting victory, surged ahead only to find themselves encircled by fresh enemy soldiers. The great mass of Roman soldiers was quickly crushed in a vice-like formation. Hannibal was to use this tactic of exhausting the opposition in their frontal assault, giving way at the center and surrounding them for the kill, throughout the long Italian campaign.

His military tactics are still being copied: Von Schlieffer, the Prussian commander of the invasion of France in 1914, studied Cannae in great detail; when Rommel drove the British Army back towards Tobruk he wrote in his diary about the lessons of Cannae; and as recently as the first Gulf War, General Norman Schwarzkopf claimed that the success of his short campaign was due to his application of principles based on Hannibal's victory.

Despite his military successes Hannibal's later years were tragic. In 203 BC he returned to defend Carthage against the Romans, but was defeated by Scipio at the Battle of Zama. After this he worked briefly as a magistrate in Carthage, proved unpopular and moved to Antioch at the eastern end of the Mediterranean. Little is known of his final years except that he was pursued relentlessly by the Romans. Most likely he took his own life to escape them and at the small town of Lybissia, near modern Gevze in Turkey, there is a small mausoleum in his memory.

———～∅∅∅～———

One of the lesser-known but most beautiful parts of the French Alps, Le Queyras is a circular basin dominated by the majestic Mont Viso, over 3,000 meters high. Unlike most other parts of the southeastern corner of France where the boundary with Savoy (now part of Italy) changed several times, Le Queyras has been entirely French since 1349, thus ensuring its people and villages a kind of cultural authenticity. It is a fascinating area in its own right quite apart from its association with Hannibal: the isolation, primitive villages and tiny farms typify much of rural France until a century ago.

In recent times sustained efforts have been made to attract visitors, largely through investment in camping and hiking infrastructure rather than hotels; so Le Queyras remains largely unspoilt. It has experienced serious depopulation but offers superb south-facing mountain and valley landscapes, around 300 days of sunshine a year and a rare tranquility. The mountains to the east are wild and rocky with screes, glassy schists, lakes and waterfalls accessible only by walking. Originally part of an ancient sea-bed, they were pushed up into a series of jagged peaks and, much later, dissected by glaciers and rivers. A tiny geological museum at Chateau Queyras has a display explaining the formation of the Alps and at Molines a tourist shop sells excellent fossils of early marine life at bargain prices.

CHATEAU QUEYRAS

The only town of significance is Guillestre. Several small villages built mainly of wood reflect an older, mountain way of life based on the rhythm of the seasons. Queyras has always been famous for its wood work especially wooden toys made during the long period of indoor living in winter. At 2,000 meters St Véran, claiming to be the highest village in Europe, has houses with huge lofts where harvests were once stored. There is an interesting church with an upper gallery for the choir and old people. Aiguilles, with its wooden houses and balconies, has a fine location surrounded by a forest of larch trees.

The most imposing structure is the fortress at Chateau Queyras built in the thirteenth century at one of the narrowest points in the lower Guil Valley so that it effectively sealed France off from attack by the Savoyards. After Hannibal fought his way through the ambush of the Guil gorge he desperately looked for a site where he could rally his soldiers. The ancient Greek historian, Polybius, who faithfully recorded the journey, refers to a huge rock that rose in the center of the valley, almost certainly where the fort now stands as the point where the Carthaginians regrouped before they tackled the Alps.

—⟦∿∿⟧—

In tracking Hannibal's journey it is possible to explore not only Le Queyras but also the high country between the Var and Ubaye Rivers and a fascinating part of the Piedmont of Italy around the towns of Bra and Alba. Le Queyras is reached from the south by taking the Autoroute du Val de Durance (A 51) through Sisteron to Gap and then the N94 to Embrun and Guillestre. Alternatively, for those who enjoy driving on mountain roads, there are the spectacular but somewhat dangerous D roads leading from the N202 over the high passes between the Var and the Ubaye Valleys.

An attractive exit from Le Queyras is to follow Hannibal's route from Molines, crossing the Alps at *Col Agnel* and then to Cuneo and Alba on the Italian plain. This journey allows a stay in Alba where it is possible to taste some of the finest Italian heavy red wines such as Barolo, Barbaresco and Dolcetto.

The white truffles of Alba are famous for their extraordinarily delicate flavor. Numerous varieties are determined by the species of oak on the roots of which they grow; but all are much sought after and extremely expensive. Unlike the black truffles of the *Côtes de Provence* wine area, white truffles are not used so directly in cooking but are shredded over a wide variety of dishes; they are also distinguished by their pungent odor that overcomes all delicate flavors. Their season is from October to March, during which time vines and trees change color and distinctive mists hug the valley floors each morning.

About half way between Bra and Alba, the attractive, medieval hotel, the *Castello di Santa Vittoria d'Alba*, is a good base from which to explore both Le Queyras and the Piedmont. Its pleasant outdoor restaurant has great views over the rolling vineyards; it has been the subject of both a book and a film called *The Secret of Santa Vittoria*. The secret refers to the storing of valuable local wine in cellars dug into the limestone hill to hide them from the German Army during the Second World War.

Valley of the Roya

Chapter Five

The Roya Valley:
From Prehistoric Art to The Salt Trade

We were lured to the Upper Roya Valley by the promise of Bronze Age art; not the huge raging bulls and bison painted on underground cave walls at Lascaux but small engravings on red rock out in the open air. Since 2000 BC hundreds of people have engraved their interpretations of life here, around the magical Mount Bego beside the Roya River. Add to this the landforms honed by ancient glaciers, the herds of rare animals, the spectacular larch forests as well as the knowledgeable guide who led us through these marvels in the Mercantour National Park and you will understand our enthusiasm.

A first exploration not only fulfilled our expectations but brought other discoveries. As early as the Bronze Age, farmers of the Rhone Valley in the west and the Po Valley in the east apparently shared religious beliefs and since medieval times, this area has been subjected to alternating political masters – France and Italy - who brought different languages, cultures, art and architecture.

The Roya rises high in the French Alps close to Italy and flows almost directly south to reach the Mediterranean between Menton and Ventimiglia. Not far from its source is Mount Bego which at 2,700 meters above sea level looms over several high valleys: the *Fontanalba,* the *Casterine* and the *Merveilles* (Valley of the Marvels) with its unique treasury of prehistoric art.

In the Valley of the Marvels there are small rocky outcrops of both red and green schist. For centuries the green schist provided roof slates for village buildings while the red schist boulders provided the 'canvas' for ancient artists. Using dots instead of lines, their stippled engravings depict horned animals, weapons, tools, gods and, it is believed, agricultural fields. Neolithic farmers in this region learnt to forge metal. They dug into copper seams and used earth kilns to smelt the ore. By adding a little tin they produced bronze, a stronger metal that could be reheated and cast into moulds for axe-heads, spades, spoons, cups and jewelry. Bronze goods became a major form of wealth accumulation and the rock engravings illustrate these kinds of objects.

ENGRAVINGS :VALLEY OF THE MARVELS

Fertility seems to have been an important concept central to the religious beliefs of these Bronze Age people. Fertile women produced children and rain made the soil more fertile so the worship of an earth/mother goddess was widespread. The procreational role of the male was often reflected in the worship of a virile man/bull god. As metal weapons became more refined and agricultural wealth accumulated, communities grew more warlike and the male element became more significant. And many groups had religious specialists who guided the rituals associated with worship and sacrifice in sacred places such as caves, river banks, forest groves or mountain tops.

Mount Bego is forbidding, frequently rent by sudden violent thunderstorms that blot out its upper half from the valleys below. Yet on a fine day it is almost totally visible from the central square in the town of La Brigue. Farming communities made pilgrimages to the mountain for about 3,500 years through to the late medieval period. They came to worship at Mount Bego and the engravings on the red schist may have been a central feature of their worship.

Most engravings are small, less than thirty centimeters long. Although extending over a large area they tend to occur in clusters, the largest of which is in the desolate Valley of the Marvels. By far the most common subject is a horn-shaped symbol believed to represent a bull-god who was able, with thunder and lightning, to deliver the fertilizing rain. Geometrical grids represent fields of crops waiting to receive rain. Metal weapons and tools are plentiful, especially daggers. Animals are harnessed to plows so we know that farming was practised. Only a few anthropomorphic figures have been found and some of these have since been given descriptive names such as 'tribal chief', 'the sorcerer' and 'Christ'.

These engravings are of great value to our understanding of life in prehistoric times. Clearly, local people were familiar with them for centuries; witness the medieval Latin inscription in the Valley of the Marvels that has been translated as 'death to the man who seduced my brother's son'. But, as with many other parts of rural France, it was not until the early twentieth century that this rock art became widely known, and then largely due to the English botanist, Charles Bicknell who, in his search for new plants, uncovered many engravings and publicized them in scientific journals.

Vehicular access to the Valley of the Marvels is by way of an Italian-built military road, little improved since the area became part of France in 1947. Although there are many hiking paths it takes almost two hours in a four-wheel-drive vehicle to negotiate the rocky, see-saw track and then a two hour, mostly gentle, uphill walk to reach the engravings. Opening times are restricted by snow but generally extend from mid-June to early October.

Access to Fontanalba Valley is much easier and while it has fewer engravings the animal life is more plentiful. Among others there are marmots, chamois, ibex, wild boar, golden eagles and bearded vultures. No wonder the Savoy kings used the area as a private hunting reserve. Spring flowers include gentian violets, rhododendrons, edelweiss and almost seventy species of orchids; in autumn the larch forest becomes an intense yellow mass. In 1979 both valleys were incorporated into the newly created Mercantour National Park, covering 68,000 hectares, now considered one of Europe's finest natural reserves. A key policy of the park management has been to restore the original flora and fauna despite some reservations from local sheep farmers who feared that the re-introduction of wolves, for example, would threaten their flocks.

MARMOT   IBEX

Before seeing the engravings *in situ* it is worth spending an hour or two in the little Museum of Merveilles in Tende. The museum's architecture is quite striking: stark white columns are spattered with a pattern of figures based on the ancient engravings while the forefront is paved in green schist. Inside, the museum is human in scale yet incorporates the latest in display technology. There is one relatively large original engraving, 'chief of the tribe', with accurate copies of a host of others. The exhibits are clearly linked to the physical environment and long-term pastoral traditions. One popular exhibit is the 'talking man', a lifelike replica that can be programmed to tell stories about shepherds who spent summers with their sheep in the high valleys or to recount local legends. It speaks in French, Italian, English and German.

Our first visit to the 'marvels' was in July, 2001. We took advantage of the special scheme organized by local hotels for a two–night stay with an all-day excursion to the engravings. We were fortunate in our choice of hotel: *Le Mirval* in La Brigue. Monsieur Amédée Dellepiane, one of its owners, is a most experienced guide who was able, in a mixture of French and English, with charm and wit, to coax us over the rough terrain. Our bedroom looked out to the mountains and a fast-flowing stream that supplied fresh trout for dinner.

—————

Salt has been traded over long distances since prehistoric times. Its value lies as a preservative and tanning agent and as a vital component of human and animal diets. For southeastern France the major source was saline marshes of the Rhone Delta from where sailing barges carried the salt to Nice. After unloading came an arduous journey by mule over mountainous tracks through the Roya Valley to the Piedmont Plain and Turin, a journey known as the *Route du Sel.*

Early stories tell of brigands along the route who stole the valuable cargo or kidnapped its wealthy merchants for ransom. After the rulers of Savoy acquired the Piedmont (moving their capital to Turin) they controlled some of the salt road, but the Counts of Tende (the Lascaris) demanded exorbitant taxes for right-of-passage. When Savoy endowed Nice with the status of a free port the salt trade increased sharply and the Lascaris allied themselves to their powerful Savoyard neighbour who then policed most of the *Route du Sel* from Escarene to Sospel, Breil-sur-Roya, Saorge, Tende and over the high col to Turin. Most villages were fortified and the ancient towns of Saorge and Tende had striking hillside locations commanding strategic views of the valleys and gorges.

Towards the end of the eighteenth century there were something like 15,000 mules carrying around 5,000 tonnes of salt each year, while on their return journey they brought wool from the sheep of the lush alpine pastures and rice from the Piedmont. The mules were mountain-bred for toughness to cope with the loads, cold weather and difficult tracks – as were the muleteers. But even they couldn't satisfy the demand for salt. Tracks were widened and surfaced to allow the use of carts and carriages yet they still had to negotiate the 2,000 meters high *Col de Tende* that often could not be used in winter.

When the Roya Valley periodically fell into French hands the salt trade declined as happened during the reign of Napoleon but after his final defeat in 1815 the Savoyard overseers restored stability. Yet external factors were changing: the port of Genoa became part of Savoy and provided an alternative route for the salt and it became possible to produce industrial salt close to the market. So the salt route today is essentially a tourist route.

—◦◦◦—

Relations between French and Italian political entities in the Roya Valley have been fraught with tensions for hundreds of years. Towns were located to watch for military movements and forts constructed for quick response to imminent invasion; battles were fought and alliances forged to achieve the transfer of territory from one side of the border to the other. These tensions continued right up to the second world war.

Around the twelfth century the French political unit with the most substantial stake in this border issue was the County of Provence. Yet in the fourteenth century when the papacy shifted from Rome to Avignon for roughly a hundred years, Italian influences grew dramatically. But soon most of Provence was incorporated into the kingdom of France. Increasingly, under kings, revolutionary councils, emperors and republican presidents, Provence was drawn into a more centralized administration climaxing in the French defense policies and fortifications in the Roya Valley prior to the 1940s. The dominant Italian player in these same border issues was the old House of Savoy. It wasn't until 1870 that the state of Italy as we know it emerged and Savoy became its ruling house.

One of the most contentious stretches of border was that of the County of Nice, close to the mouth of the Roya. After centuries of rule by the counts of Provence, a tortuous to-and-fro process began. In the 1400s the Nicois allied themselves to the Duke of Savoy who later made the town a free port, abolishing customs duties and other taxes, thus bringing prosperity from increased trade. In 1793 Napoleon Bonaparte was instrumental in Nice becoming French again but after his defeat at Waterloo the city was returned to Savoy. Years later a deal was done between Emperor Louis-Napoleon, nephew of the former emperor, and Cavour, the statesman representing Savoy: in return for the promise of assistance against an Austrian invasion, Savoy would restore Nice to France. To ratify the deal a plebiscite was held in which the Nicois voted overwhelmingly to support this final change of nationality to become French in 1860.

Somewhat similar events occurred in the other contentious frontier zone of the region: around the towns of Tende and La Brigue in the high Roya Valley. The protagonists were, on the one side, the Lascari family of local feudal lords, then the duchy of Savoy and then unified Italy. On the other side was the County of Provence and then the Kingdom of France itself. The Lascaris were in conflict not only with Tende and La Brigue, but also with the other Roya towns of Saorge, Breil and Sospel. Controlling the high valley, they were long-time enemies of France. Again it was Napoleon Bonaparte who annexed the area for France but after Waterloo it was returned to Savoy. Just as in the case of the County of Nice, Cavour and Louis-Napoleon agreed that the two towns revert to France. In this case, however, the plebiscite result was aborted because not enough eligible voters turned out to vote; so Tende and La Brigue remained Savoyard. Not until after Italy's defeat in World War II did the two towns become French again.

In both the northern and southern Roya Valley the definitive symbols of recent French/Italian confrontations are the monumental forts. For the French the strategic importance of its southeastern frontier had been recognized back in the seventeenth century when Vauban designed several fortress towns near the Roya region. Much later some existing forts were strengthened and new ones built as part of the Maginot Line. Today several of them lie in ruins but a few have been restored and are open for inspection; for example, Fort St Roch near Sospel. They provide intriguing insights into military life, both above and below ground level.

Across the frontier in Italy the most substantial forts are perched high on the mountain crests near the *Col de Tende* where they could protect access to Turin. And Mussolini's two incredibly grand railway stations at the quite small towns of Breil-sur- Roya and St Dalmas-de-Tende may have been part of his dream to invade France from this direction.

⸻〰⸻

Over a long period then, the Roya Valley was the path along which people, goods and culture moved. It is an easy matter now to travel this route from Nice to the *Col de Tende* on the French-Italian border although some of the roads are winding and steep, hemmed in by a narrow gorge or a circle of high crests. Nevertheless the sense of history, the mix of mountain, rural and urban landscapes, as well as the sheer beauty of the environment more than compensate.

There is a little train that travels from Nice to Tende and sometimes to Turin; the trip to Tende takes less than two hours and starts from the main railway station in Nice. Yet there is a major advantage in going by car: watching the scenery from the train is quite restricted by the long tunnels – up to six kilometers. Whether by car or train we strongly recommend staying at least two nights in La Brigue, Tende or St Dalmas-de-Tende. This allows time to sample a few of the unique attractions of Mercantour National Park: its rock art, larch forests and some of its wild animals. Arrangements for guided tours can be made by tourist offices or by hotels.

A purist following the salt route would begin a few kilometers east of Nice at Villefranche, the free port that was so important to the salt trade. But this beautiful harbor now contains little apart from luxury yachts and the occasional ocean liner, so go north and drive past the large perched village of Escarene for the climb up to the *Col de Braus*, and then a winding descent into Sospel. It was on this downward stretch that we learnt the meaning of lacet, a shoelace or hairpin bend - and there were eighteen of them! An easier route begins at Ventimiglia.

About fifteen kilometers south of Sospel the fortress of St Roch is heralded by old canons close to the main road. Sospel sits astride the Bevera River, a tributary of the Roya. Because of the ring of mountains it has a seemingly impregnable location; even towards the end of the Second World War the Germans held out here despite heavy Allied bombing. Subsequently the severe damage has been repaired so the former eleventh century bridge, for example, again has its clock tower that once functioned as the tollgate where salt-laden mule caravans were taxed for passage through local territory. Other attractions include the town's arcaded houses, fountains and churches; in particular, *l'Eglise St-Michel* has a Romanesque bell-tower with Lombard stripes, a simplicity later modified by huge glowing altarpieces in Baroque style. Sospel is now a sunny market town with welcoming riverside cafes.

Again with many lacets, it's up to the *Col de Brouis* and down to join the national road (N204) that runs gently along the valley floor. Just south of this intersection Breil-sur-Roya sits beside a large peaceful dam. Clearly visible from the main road is the large *Ste-Maria-en-Albis*, an eighteenth century church of fine proportions, a Baroque interior and a huge crack in its wall from damage in the last war.

At Fontan a short detour leads to Saorge, a large village with one of the most striking settings in southeastern France. It was a Roman colony and a secure stronghold throughout the Middle Ages, standing high above the valley floor and looking south through the gorge for any approaching army. Nevertheless it was captured by Napoleon's

SAORGE

troops in the 1790s and again by the French in World War II. Its curving streets cut into the hillside with three rows of closely packed Italianate houses: green shutters and decorated entrances line the stepped streets and pedestrian archways. The Franciscan Monastery at the eastern end of the village is a Baroque building among the olive groves, with a good view over the gorge. Further east still is a simple eleventh century chapel to the *Madonna del Poggia*.

Back on the main road, a few kilometers further on is the turn-off to La Brigue, in rich farmland on narrow floodplains. It is a small town that has much to offer the traveler: medieval green schist houses, carved lintels and significant religious buildings. A Romanesque church, the *Collégiale Saint-Martin*, has Lombardy panels on its facade, notable primitive paintings from the Nice School and a remodelled interior of Baroque gilding with an organ. Two Baroque chapels nearby also demonstrate Italian influences on their architecture. La Brigue is altogether a cheerful town whose ambience is one of considerable past wealth from the salt and wool trade.

Almost four kilometers east of La Brigue, past an attractive medieval bridge, is the *Chapelle Notre-Dame-des-Fontaines*. The *fontaines* are springs whose miraculous powers have drawn pilgrims since the twelfth century and the oldest section of the little building dates from this time. The chapel owes much to the tranquility of its natural setting: trickling streams and tall shady trees. In contrast the interior glows with striking frescoes of dancing figures and scenes from the life of Christ painted by 15th century artists.

NOTRE-DAME-DES-FONTAINES

In earlier times religious artists and architects were often itinerants whose work was financed by small rural communities that had great amounts of faith but little money. But in the face of reformist tendencies within the Catholic Church, villagers wanted to encourage others to hold firm in their beliefs. Frequently the simple chapels were sited along roads and tracks to carry the message to merchants, pilgrims and other travelers.

As trade increased many communities prospered and built grand churches or redecorated older ones in extravagant Baroque style. After the Protestant Reform, followers of the Catholic Church set out to prove that nothing was too beautiful or too expensive for God. Building facades had pediments, intricate roof lines and marble statues; inside there might be gold statues, fluted columns, inlaid marble stairs, dazzling altarpieces and, later, large organs. The *Chapelle Notre-Dame-des-Fontaines* broadly conforms to this arrangement: an almost bare twelfth century exterior with a rich fifteenth century interior of vibrant frescoes that illustrate the life of Christ. They cover most of the walls and ceiling such that this little church has been called the 'Sistine Chapel of the southern Alps'.

Almost surrounded by mountains and with multi-level houses that cling to the curving, rocky terrain, Tende is another Italianate town – larger than Saorge and spilling down to the River Roya itself. The buildings date mainly from the fourteenth century when La Brigue and Tende were ruled by the Lascari family. An important staging point on the *Route du Sel,* Tende leads to the mountain pass at 2,000 meters, probably the toughest slopes for the mules carrying salt between Nice and Turin. A tunnel has replaced the torturous track but it is now an inadequate, alternating one-way road for vehicular traffic between France and Italy. Several military buildings demonstrate the strategic importance of the pass.

Some of the Lascari family are buried at the little cemetery in Tende while others lie in the *Collégiale Notre-Dame-de-l'Assomption,* locally called 'the Cathedral'. Despite a map from the tourist office showing its location at the southern end of town near the Nice Gate, the church is difficult to find. We strongly recommend perseverance as it is a stunning example of early Baroque building. The exterior is ablaze with a joyous design in pink, yellow and blue, while the interior has a curved blue ceiling with frescoes and stonework, as well as a spectacular apse embellished with glowing precious metals.

TENDE: THE NICE GATE

Now the prime function of Tende is tourism, focussing on its proximity to the Mercantour National Park and its numerous walking tracks. The town is fun to explore, people are friendly, the food is simple but good and there are quality hotels: *Le Chamois d'Or du Center* on *Place Republique*, nearby *Le Prieuré* in St-Dalmas-de-Tende and *Le Mirval* in La Brigue.

VAUBAN'S RING OF FORTRESSES

Chapter Six

Vauban's Great Fortresses

Since prehistoric times communities have had to find ways of defending their territory. Early on they recognized the crucial importance of location, often siting their villages on hilltops, hillsides, cliff-edges or at the head of a gorge. Gradually walls became more significant, evolving from simple timber barricades to the crenallated stone ramparts of later centuries. This chapter describes one man's innovative designs: a series of monumental fortresses in southeastern France. He was Sebastien le Prestre de Vauban, distinguished French soldier and foremost military engineer of the seventeenth century. He planned a line of twelve fortresses from Antibes on the Mediterranean coast, stretching inland to Entrevaux, Colmars, Sisteron, Queyras and to a cluster around Briançon in the high Alps. Of the160 forts for which he was responsible throughout France those in the southeast are considered to be some of his finest and are excellent examples of how distinguished buildings bring otherwise obscure places to life. Many can be seen today along the mountain roads north of Nice and are in uniformly good condition complete with arsenals, hospitals, kitchens, churches and map rooms.

For hundreds of years the French were obsessed with the need to protect their borders against invasion from the east: from Savoy, later to become part of Italy. The Dukes of Savoy were particularly aggressive and it was their attack in 1692 that encouraged Louis XIV to call on

Vauban. The French king had been enormously impressed by his earlier work and provided virtually unlimited resources to stop any future Savoyard invasions.

VAUBAN

Vauban was an unusual soldier. Born a commoner he quickly worked his way up through the ranks because of his skill in building new fortifications that were highly effective against sieges. This was necessary as the old medieval forts that appeared so impregnable were virtually useless in a new kind of warfare where sieges became of paramount importance. Attempts to modify the old buildings by making the walls thicker and towers taller simply provided a better target for improved mortars and cannon, lessons Vauban had learned from his earlier experience.

New forms of military technology, therefore, as well as better organized armies presented a major challenge to Vauban. His first response was to build a network of two parallel lines of forts, creating a space within which the French army could maneuver strategically and where an invader could become bogged down. This space was known as the *pré carré*, or dueling field, and the technique referred to as 'siege by parallel'. These strategies were applied around Calais, Dunkirk and Lille where the land was very flat.

The rugged topography of southeastern France however necessitated a different response. Vauban continued to believe in the need for a system or network of forts but location now became a more important consideration. He had to construct fortresses that not only supported each other along a defensive line but protected those areas most vulnerable to attack: the river valleys and mountain passes. To this art of positioning he brought the additional skills of an outstanding engineer who had built bridges, canals, and harbors all over France. He became the master of the star-shaped fort with straight-sided moats, lined with walls built of local material. Bastions protruded from the walls to maximize the defenders' line of fire and to minimize the area exposed to the enemy. He left no blind spots where an attacker could hide. Covered walkways protected the defending soldiers who could fire on the enemy with cannon from behind thick walls and rake the moats with handguns from slits in the walls.

In 1692 the King wanted to concentrate on the borderlands between France and Savoy, however Vauban considered the threat to the entire south of France so great that he decided to construct a semi-circle of twelve strongholds known as *la corset des forteresses*, like a tight brace to enclose Savoy and protect France from invasion. Sometimes he started building from scratch, other times from existing structures and usually in river valleys. When Vauban received the King's instructions the Savoyards were pushing into France where it was most vulnerable at the *Col de Montgenèvre*, one of the easiest passes in the Alps near the old town of Briançon which therefore became the immediate focus of attention.

⸻ ༄ ⸻

High in the Alps, only fifteen kilometers from the border and at the junction of five streams it is not surprising that Briançon was a military town for most of its existence. Initially fortified by the Romans to guard their trade route from Milan to Vienne, its history has been dominated by wars and the building of defensive installations. Nowadays, in summer Briançon is full of traffic leading into Italy and in winter covered with snow, but its claim to fame is the mountainous setting and the unique mass of fortifications built over 300 years.

The town is divided into two parts. The upper one, rebuilt by Vauban, was surrounded by walls, inside which he constructed the *Fort du Château* that dominates the town. Still there today these walls have only four entrances, each opening onto a drawbridge across the old moat. The houses built within the walls have five levels and the streets are long and narrow with many fountains. The *Place d'Armes*, a bright central square, has two fine sundials one bearing the intriguing inscription 'Life slips by like a shadow'.

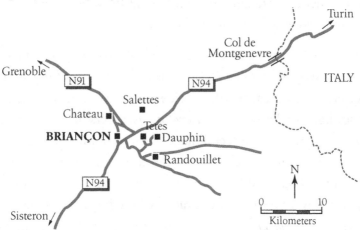

FORTS AROUND BRIANCON

Next, Vauban planned and constructed an interconnected ring of four imposing forts around Briancon to reinforce this central *Fort du Château*. The largest and most important, the *Fort des Têtes*, was not completed until 1725. Covering an area larger than the town itself the building could hold 1250 soldiers comfortably and, in times of siege, the entire population of the town. With this possibility in mind Vauban designed a long covered bridge to link the town to the fort.

The *Fort des Salettes*, probably the best preserved of all his forts in this area, was built specifically to guard the pass into Savoy and prevent invaders gaining a dominant position above the town. A menacing building, it broods over Briançon and the Durance Valley and, with the support of *Fort Dauphin*, the third fort in the group, it could block the route from Italy into France.

Finally, the *Fort de Randouillet* designed to protect the all-important *Fort des Têtes* from attack, completed his defensive ring of forts. How successful was this huge enterprise? Its major test came in 1815 when the forts were surrounded by allied forces led by the Austrians yet survived the siege which lasted three months until the Treaty of Paris was signed.

This system of strongholds continued to be used until the end of the second world war and is now a major tourist attraction. As well there are many walks and drives into the quite spectacular mountain landscapes around Briancon, including the lovely Queyras region and the *Parc des Ecrins*. Less well-known is the huge natural fortress, a limestone mass, known as *Vercors*, famous as a stronghold for French resistance fighters.

⟆ⱷⱷ⟆

After Briançon Vauban moved south following the Durance River, the great transverse tributary of the Rhone and a major gateway linking Savoy with southern France. Close to the Italian border the Guil, a small, fast-flowing tributary of the Durance, was of critical importance. This is the valley where Hannibal led his huge army over the Alps and where Caesar took his soldiers from Rome into central Europe.

By 1692 Savoy had already captured the nearby towns of Guillestre, Embrun and Gap and there was an urgent need for French defensive action. The enormous star-shaped fort built by Vauban on Mont-Dauphin guarded the Durance and Guil valleys until the French army vacated it in 1980. More a fortified town than a fortress it was built from local pink marble consistent with his wish to include aesthetic considerations in the design of his buildings. On an inhospitable wind-swept plateau and perched above the confluence of the two rivers even today it appears impregnable. Inside, the residential village of Mont-Dauphin contains barracks, an arsenal, artillery and cavalry spaces, a hotel, *mairie*, shops and restaurants. The entire complex, which could accommodate over 2,000 soldiers, is surrounded by massive walls and moats in near-perfect condition. Tours along the ramparts provide excellent views of the Guil Gorge where Hannibal was ambushed 2,000 years before.

———

The high valley of Queyras, one of the most isolated and beautiful parts of the French Alps, has for centuries served as an artery linking Italy with France. From medieval times the French have attempted to fortify it at its most strategic point. Here, at the village of Chateau Queyras, they had built *Fort Queyras* on a huge rock, almost certainly the place where Hannibal had gathered his soldiers after their ambush by the Gauls. It is a natural defensive location which completely blocks the valley of the Guil. Vauban transformed the old fort: he doubled its size, reinforced the walls, built an arsenal, vaults and space for artillery. As with all his forts it is most impressive when viewed from a distance: lonely, heavy and threatening, dominating but fitting into the narrow valley giving a clear warning to potential invaders. Occupied by the French army until 1967 it remains in a good state of repair.

To extend his network Vauban completely rebuilt existing forts at Colmars, Seyne and Entrevaux, each on the France-Savoy border at that time. Colmars, a good example of a fortified medieval village, is the first major settlement south of the *Col d'Allos*, an important pass through the high mountains of northern Provence. Here on the upper Verdon River the mountains give way to more open country, a natural point for invasion from the north.

COLMARS: FORT SAVOY

Vauban built a defensive wall around Colmars with two large forts, the *Fort de Savoie* and the *Fort de France*, the former being by far the most impressive and the best preserved. On a hillside at the northern end of the town, its high blank walls with protruding watch towers must have been a forbidding sight to any attackers. There are only two gates into Colmars, each at the end of a straight narrow main street that was originally connected by covered passages to the forts. Unlike most of Vauban's fortified towns it was destroyed many times, usually by the Dukes of Savoy, but each time it was rebuilt. It is all very quiet and peaceful today although the forts continue to brood over the houses and shops that cluster within the newly rebuilt walls.

Only ruins remain of Vauban's fortress perched high above the isolated little market town of Seyne, 40 kilometers north of Digne, but they demonstrate the importance of location. The fort had a commanding outlook over the wide and beautiful valley of the Blanche River, once on the French-Savoy border, now used for animal breeding and for skiing in winter. Just below the battered fortress the thirteenth century alpine Romanesque church, *Notre Dame de Nazareth*, with its fine Gothic porch and high steeple, is quite impressive.

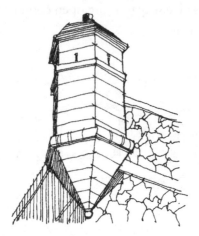

COLMARS: WATCHTOWER

Entrevaux too was a frontier post until the late nineteenth century but unlike Colmars and Seyne it was located on the Var, the major river of the entire region connecting the mountains to the sea, and was therefore of particular importance in Vauban's grand defensive plan. As with other perched villages along the Var its origins lie in the eleventh century when local people, weary of Saracen incursions from the south and river floods in spring, moved up onto the valley sides. Here they clustered in tall unadorned houses, always with an adequate supply of water and with a church used as a refuge in times of attack.

Entrevaux's site on a tilted rocky spur is quite exceptional, enabling Vauban to build his most visually striking stronghold. On one side the village was virtually impregnable from the mountains and on the other side the Var served as a deep moat. Access was via a high drawbridge guarded by two towers. Vauban built his fortress at the top of the spur and linked it to the town far below by a double-walled ramp with twenty towers that zigzag down the side of the valley. Today, the steep walk up the ramparts takes about twenty-five minutes but the reward at the top is a splendid panorama of the Var Valley. This particularly attractive town retains its medieval character of narrow streets, tall houses with balconies overlooking tiny squares and many fountains. The cathedral, incorporated into the fortifications, dates from the seventeenth century and contains fine baroque decoration.

ENTREVAUX: DRAWBRIDGE

Another important task was to strengthen the citadel that protects the prosperous city of Sisteron, regional capital of the Durance Valley. Vauban also designed new projects for the perched town of St-Paul-de-Vence. And he was active even in Grasse where his cousin, the bishop, obtained advice on the construction of the walls around the town. The remains of this work can be seen in the *Rue de l'Evéche* and the *Passage Vauban* near the medieval cathedral. At Antibes his Fort Carré, a massive star-shaped structure overlooking the site of the ancient Greek town, ceased to be strategically important in 1860 when Nice became part of France.

How successful was Vauban's line of fortresses? It was built to prevent incursions from Savoy and to stabilize the borderlands between the two countries. It may have served as a deterrent for a short time in the late seventeenth and early eighteenth centuries but intermittent warfare and border changes continued as late as 1947 when much of the area near Briançon and Tende was ceded to France. One must question, therefore, the continued emphasis on huge forts when military technology changed so quickly and diplomacy became more important in resolving border conflicts, yet the forts remain as imposing reminders of the genius of one of the greatest military engineers.

For his work in revolutionizing the design of fortresses and siege techniques Vauban was promoted to Marshal of France in 1703 by Louis XIV and then began writing on a wide range of social issues. A man with strong humanitarian values, he recommended the introduction of an equitable tax system that did not exclude the aristocracy as a way of overcoming the chronic financial crisis of the time. He also made repeated pleas for tolerance of the Protestant Huguenots. For this he fell out of favor and was banished from the court at Versailles; he died in disgrace a year later. Another century was to pass before the nation recognized his genius; Napoleon reburied his heart under the dome of the *Hôtel des Invalides* in Paris where it now rests a few meters from Napoleon himself and other military heroes.

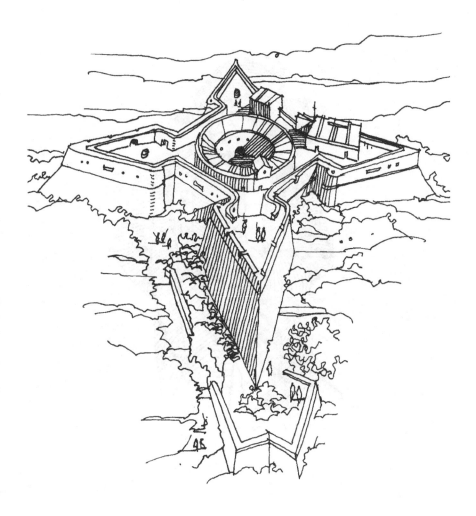

ANTIBES: FORT CARRÉ

NAPOLEON IN HIS GREY COAT

Chapter Seven

Napoleon's Flight from Elba

From Cannes to Grenoble a section of the national highway, N85, is called the Route Napoleon. Opened in 1932 it follows the path taken by the ex-emperor in 1815 through southeastern France after his escape from the tiny island of Elba. This journey was part of the final 100 days during which he briefly again experienced glory, before defeat at Waterloo. Little has been written about it but today there are clues along the route that help to track his remarkable expedition over the Martime Alps.

Like Hannibal, the great Carthaginian general who led an army over the Alps some 2,000 years before, Napoleon had to move with stealth and speed to prevent enemy intelligence being aware of his movements. He knew about Hannibal, referring to him as one of the 'Great Captains' of the past from whom he had learnt much about military campaigns. But while Hannibal took roughly five weeks to travel from the Durance River to the Po Valley in Italy, Napoleon completed his journey of roughly the same distance, from Grasse to Grenoble in seven days. Admittedly, Hannibal had over 100,000 men – infantry and cavalry –and 37 elephants with higher mountains to traverse. But Napoleon, too, had difficult terrain over which to take his few hundred men who with mules and a few horses were forced to carry heavy loads in bitter winter conditions. Moreover, the two generals had different motivations.

Hannibal was obsessed with invading, fighting and ultimately destroying Rome. Napoleon, on the other hand, believed emphatically that his journey was 'a rightful return to power at the behest of the French people' and ordered that not a shot should be fired.

As one of his enemies once said, Napoleon could move with the speed of lightning. He did this not just on the ground with his soldiers but also in his military career. At the age of 24 in 1793 he was promoted from his post as artillery officer in the Revolutionary Army to that of brigadier-general for his successful contribution to the capture of Toulon from the British. Two years later he used 'a whiff of grapeshot' to subdue a rebellion in Paris and was rewarded by appointment as Commander-in-Chief to the Army of the Interior. Then as General Napoleon, he led his troops to victory in northern Italy thus containing Austrian expansion.

After less successful expeditions to Egypt and the Middle East he returned to Paris where he took advantage of his growing popularity. Severe financial problems were confronting the revolutionary government and an incredible reign of terror held sway, including frequent use of the guillotine. Napoleon helped organize a coup that enabled him to become the powerful First Consul of the Republic; his military successes continued but he now began to develop an efficient administrative system for the entire nation; one in which centralized power replaced the highly fragmented institutional structures of pre-revolutionary France. Reforms were made to the taxation and monetary system, to education and to law courts. In fact, much of the legal framework within which the nation still operates was laid down in the Code Napoleon.

In 1804 Napoleon, only 35 years old, proclaimed himself Emperor of France. During the next decade his Grande Armée enlarged the French Empire substantially, subduing the major European powers. Only Britain with its superior navy remained an active aggressor. At the Battle of

Austerlitz 75,000 French troops soundly defeated 90,000 Austrian and Russian troops in one day. After this great victory Napoleon appeared to be invincible.

Almost a decade later though, his disastrous Russian experience was a sign of impending doom. After barely winning the major battle against the Russians at Borodino he lost the war: he was unable to initiate peace negotiations with the Tsar who with his supporters had left Moscow deserted and in flames. While Napoleon sought solutions to this unusual tactical maneuver the French army waited for five weeks decimated by exhaustion, starvation, guerilla attacks by the Cossacks and the onset of a fierce winter. From an army of 600,000 men many died or deserted; very few returned to France. Austria, Prussia and Russia converged on Paris. Facing defeat at last, Napoleon abdicated in 1814 accepting exile to become ruler of Elba and accepting also the restoration of the French monarchy.

The trip from Paris to Elba was devastating for Napoleon. Many people mourned the loss of family and friends on the battlefields, taxes to finance the wars had been harsh and even his trusted marshals abandoned him. In the south of France where the monarchy had much support, feelings against him were particularly strong. Life on Elba was depressing and he soon began planning his escape. The only ship available had to be disguised as British, provisioned for three months and had almost no room for horses. Nevertheless, ten months after his arrival he set sail for France and the re-conquest of his empire. So began the dramatic journey across the French Alps toward Grenoble and then Paris where he could, he believed, raise another huge army that would defeat his enemies and restore France to its exalted position with an empire second only to that of the ancient Romans.

When the European powers congregated in Vienna to divide the spoils from his Russian defeat, they faced a dilemma: how would France be apportioned among the victors yet be retained in some form so as not to invite rebellion? Although this was a serious occasion there was much celebration for the defeat of a feared tyrant. During the prolonged negotiationss, however, the participants learned of Napoleon's escape from Elba and consternation broke out. How could the great powers again face an amazing military intelligence with such speed of movement?

Today his passage to Grenoble is easy to follow on the N85. Most towns herald the path of the deposed leader and his bedraggled soldiers. Columns, plaques, statues and inscriptions provide a strong sense of history, especially as many of the small towns have not changed much over the past 190 years. What follows now is a day-to-day account of the trek through southeastern France using data from the helpful tourist office in Grasse.

1st March 1815
Late in the afternoon Napoleon and his men landed on a beach at Golfe-Juan near Antibes, far away from Marseilles where a large garrison of royalist troops was stationed. An unpretentious obelisk of blue mosaic on the Quai du Port near the tourist office celebrates the landing. Like several other monuments along the way it carries a flying eagle: he was to be the eagle that would fly from one bell-tower to another until he reached the towers of Notre Dame Cathedral in Paris. Some of his men were arrested so the group moved on to sleep near the beach at Cannes, only a few kilometers away. But even here it would be difficult to withhold news of the landing from authorities in Paris and there was no evidence of any local support so Napoleon then made the firm decision that despite the harsh winter conditions in the mountains he would keep to the back roads and avoid the much easier trek up the Rhone Valley.

2nd March 1815
Still anxious not to advertize his whereabouts, around 1a.m. Napoleon and his troops struggled up toward Grasse. When the town's alarm bell

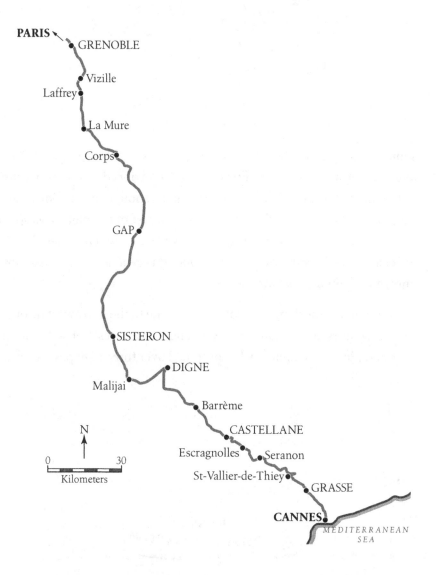

LA ROUTE NAPOLEON

THE FLYING EAGLE

sounded he feared a hostile reception but the locals were untroubled and even brought wine and flowers. They convinced him that because of the difficult terrain ahead the few big guns should be abandoned and that mules should carry the provisions. The rest of the night was spent on the little plateau of Roquevignon above Grasse where today there is a small snack-bar with views to the Mediterranean and a tall tree, now known as 'Napoleon's Oak'.

Later in the morning they followed a route to the northwest through rugged countryside of bare limestone and dense forests of spiky holm-oaks and pines. The mule tracks continued over three high passes—some

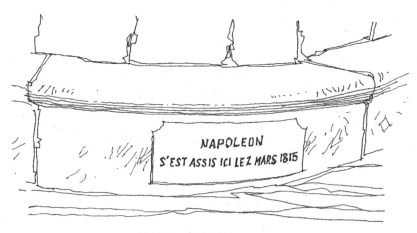

THE SEAT AT ST-VALLIER-DE-THEY

up to 1,000 meters. To negotiate the precipitous paths the soldiers and mules often had to walk in single file. Then it was down to the pretty little town of St-Vallier-de Thiey where the ex-emperor rested on a stone bench under a plane tree in the central square, *Place de la Liberation.*

On through Escragnolles the country became less hospitable. Today there are a few small perfume distilleries and just before Seranon the lovely *Chapelle de Notre Dame de Gratimoine* stands in grand isolation. Napoleon stayed the night in Seranon at Brondet Castle, now in ruins.

3rd March 1815

Next morning, after a breakfast of broth at the nearby inn, the *Logis de Pin,* part of which remains, they marched on through a fairly mountainous area of pine forests and bare rock. Their goal was lunch at Castellane. Today it is worth walking around this ancient town to appreciate its dramatic setting: nestling against a limestone cliff with the spectacular *Chapelle-Notre-Dame-du-Roc* overlooking the ruins of Roman and medieval settlements and a bridge across the Verdon River. Parts of the fourteenth century walls remain, one gate supporting a sturdy clock tower. On the northern edge of the town, the *Musée de le Résistance* reminds us that the Maquis was especially active in the nearby Verdon Gorge during the second world war. The local administrative office, now the Ethnological Museum, at 34 Rue National, welcomed the ex-emperor to lunch.

Many of the valleys here run in a north-south direction but in the Pre-Alps of Castellane (and of Digne further north) they are cut by transverse gorges that required steeper climbs. Generally it was very difficult terrain where the mule tracks crossed stony *garrigue,* skirting limestone boulders and deep canyons. There were, of course, very few inhabitants. That night Napoleon slept in a judge's house at Barrème.

4th March 1815

Having walked some 150 kilometers the men, mules and horses were exhausted but along with their leader the soldiers trudged on through deep snow carrying provisions, equipment and saddles. News of the troops descending on Paris had spread. Local authorities had planned to halt the procession at Digne-les-Bains hoping that the citizens would block the rebels but there was little opposition. Napoleon called in at the Petit-Palace Hotel before going on to sleep at the elegant eighteenth century chateau at Malijai, one entrance to which still carries his name. It is in the center of town beside a peaceful river and is now the *mairie*.

5th March 1815

With the more rugged country now behind them, the weather also improved and the road was in better condition. Originally a Roman highway, it runs along the wide valley of the Durance River now densely-settled with farming on fertile, irrigated soils and famous for producing the most tender lamb in France. Ahead lay the large commercial center of Sisteron where Napoleon wanted to occupy the bridge over the Durance to prevent its destruction which would have greatly delayed his progress. He needn't have worried. The locals came to cheer him and the mayor provided food and drink for the men. In the center of town the thirteenth century citadel overlooks colorful streets where at 64 *Rue de Saunerie*, the old *hostellerie of le Bras d'Or* (the Golden Arm), the ex-emperor enjoyed his lunch. The *Grand Hôtel du Cours* in the center of town is comfortable, with good food, but ask for a room at the rear.

Travelling by coach at last, he quickly pressed on to the town of Gap where the crowd's reception was even more enthusiastic. Beating drums, singing and dancing, they clearly demonstrated their joyous mood. Napoleon stayed at the Marchand Hotel which no longer exists but the building replacing it bears a bright mural of the rebel group on its external wall. Gap is a good place to break the journey north: large and lively with an old street pattern but few ancient buildings because of war-time destruction. Its museum has a fine archeological

WELCOME AT GAP

collection. We stayed at the modest, well-run and soundproofed *Porte Colombe Hotel* in the *Place d'Euzières*. Napoleon left Gap the following afternoon amid cheers of support. This town was a major turning point in his return journey; he long remembered his hearty welcome from the citizens and in his will provided funds for refuges to be built in the high mountains of the nearby alpine region.

6th March 1815

This was a quiet day. Napoleon and his rapidly growing number of supporters arrived at the ancient village of Corps where he spent the night at the Palace Hotel.

7th March 1815

Having received another triumphant welcome at La Mure the group moved toward Grenoble. On the way, at Laffrey, his encounter with a government battalion has contributed to Napoleon's legendary ability to capitalize on the mood of an army. When ordered to fire at their former leader the royalist troops hesitated. At the front of the men Napoleon unbuttoned his heavy grey coat, daring anyone to shoot. Still no one moved. A moment later cheers broke out and cries of *'Vive l'Empereur'*. Many royalist soldiers then rallied to Napoleon's band of followers. He called this meeting place, *Prairie de la Rencontre*, the episode recognized today with a fine statue of him on horseback and a flying eagle plaque.

Back on the road north the enlarged group passed but didn't visit the nearby *Château Vizille*. A sixteenth century chateau, it has tall towers, a beautiful external staircase and a large serene park with lake and swans. Its fame though, stems from its important role prior to the French Revolution of 1789. A year before, some 500 members of the aristocracy, clergy and lower classes met there to challenge the way that Louis XVI had overturned Parliament and to demand freedom for every citizen. These crucial events, well presented in the chateau's large museum, paved the way for the revolution that began Napoleon's rise to power.

Many peasants joined the walk to Grenoble with flaming torches and pitchforks. Inside the city were five regiments of royalists with plenty of ammunition. The strong city gates were bolted and riflemen waited on the ramparts. When the column of rebels reached the city any gunfire was drowned by the cheering crowds, both outside and inside the walls. Improvized battering rams eventually splintered the gate and at 11 p.m. Napoleon entered a city that appeared to be entirely on his side. With immense relief he decided to rest his raggle-taggle army, some of whom had traveled on foot in bleak conditions over 300 kilometers in seven days but virtually nothing remains in Grenoble to recall these exciting events.

From then on the route through Lyon to Paris was practically downhill all the way. Despite attempts by royalist generals to halt or even delay the march its progress was unrelenting. In every town welcoming crowds lined the streets and troops from the royalist side defected. Greatly enlarged to around 20,000 Napoleon's army arrived in the capital on 20th March to find that the King had fled Paris in darkness shortly before. The forty-six year old leader believed he would now be able to recreate the glorious French Empire. Although the journey from Antibes to Paris had taken only three weeks it had been an arduous one. Restored as Emperor, Napoleon again moved quickly; only three months later his *Grande Armée* met the forces of Austria, Prussia, Russia and Britain on a Belgian plain at Waterloo. He would probably have been exhausted, physically if not mentally, by the flight from Elba so it was a confrontation between one weary general with a hastily assembled army fighting against a superbly organized and rested force of several nations led by the Duke of Wellington, who later acknowledged that it was a 'close call'. The French lost the battle and Napoleon was exiled to St Helena, an island in the south Atlantic, where he died in 1821. His body has since been returned to Paris where it now lies in the *Hôtel des Invalides*.

———

After following Napoleon's journey it is possible to return from Grenoble to Nice by taking a spectacular, if somewhat lengthy, detour southwest of the Route Napoleon. The key drawcards are the Roman ruins at Riez, the pottery center of Moustiers-Sainte-Marie and the breathtaking canyon carved by the Verdon River. This route leads to Castellane and Nice.

Follow the N85 south of Digne and branch off toward Riez. Along the way you cross the wind-swept Valensole Plateau where almond blossoms abound in March, and in July, lavender farms become a purple sea. Apparently the hilltop beside the old town of Riez was occupied by Celts and Ligurians but the Romans settled on the plain nearby. Many ancient buildings were destroyed by Huguenots and Catholics in the Wars of Religion during the sixteenth century yet there are some medieval relics including the clock tower, the town hall and houses along the *Grande-Rue*. In a meadow on the western edge of town are the remains of the first century AD temple of Apollo – four granite columns topped with marble. Close to the stream is the ancient square-shaped baptistery, dating from the fifth century, whose museum contains inscriptions, stone coffins and mosaics found on the site.

RIEZ-ROMAN RUINS

Moustiers-Sainte-Marie is a picturesque center in a beautiful setting but overflowing with tourists most of the time. The settlement grew around a fifth century monastery at the foot of limestone cliffs. Climbing the steep steps one is rewarded by the twelfth century chapel to *Notre Dame-de-Beauvoir* and by the *Château de Trigance*, now a luxury hotel. High above the chapel is a large gold star glittering in the sunlight, placed there by a crusader knight thanking God for his escape from a Jerusalem prison. In the seventeenth century the town became famous for its delicately painted ceramics of which there are many modern reproductions for sale. The *Musée de la Faience* gives a good account of the development of this industry.

South of Moustiers, past the *Lac de Ste-Croix*, the Verdon Gorge provides a spectacle often ranked alongside the Grand Canyon in the United States. It is really a series of gorges varying in depth from 250 to 700 meters cut in the limestone plateau by the metallic-green Verdon River. In a breathtaking drive of 154 kilometers, considered by some an exhilarating circuit but by others a `white knuckle' nightmare, it is possible to circumnavigate the canyon. For those who suffer from vertigo the trip along the northern edges gives an easier snapshot of these gorges. Surprisingly they became known to the outside world only about 100 years ago when Edouard Martel, commissioned to study the hydrology of the region, revealed what he called 'the American wonder of France' in the proceedings of the French Geographical Society. The discovery of what was known to local peasants for hundreds of years is indicative of the slowness with which the French themselves got to know their own country.

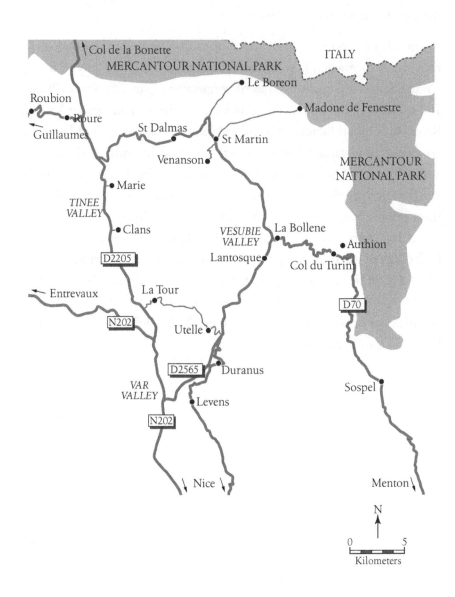

VÉSUBIE AND TINÉE VALLEYS

Chapter Eight

La Suisse Nicoise:
Vesubie's Alpine Landscapes

Some twenty kilometers north of Nice Airport along the N202, the D2565 branches off to the northeast. This road leads to the Vésubie Valley, suddenly transporting the traveler from the open broad valley of the Var to a deep, narrow, rather dark and gloomy gorge. Soon jagged peaks and cliffs rise directly from the river and the old road, in some places overhanging them so as to give an almost claustrophobic effect. Dark green conifers clinging to the sides of the cliffs add to the feeling of enclosure in the lower valley. Further up the valley toward St. Martin however the limestone cliffs and overlapping spurs give way to more open forest and lush summer pastures fed by melting snows. Travelers to the Vésubie should not expect to see grand castles or opulent baroque cathedrals; instead they should look for great forests of larch trees, ancient pilgrimage sites, isolated perched villages and relics of military installations as well as breathtaking views over distant sea and mountains.

The abrupt junction between the narrow coastal plain and the highlands was formed millions of years ago when the whole planet was cooling. Shrinkage in the Earth's crust pushed surface rocks into folds, but later the region subsided to create a seabed larger than the Mediterranean is today. Marine life flourished and its remains piled into layers, hundreds of meters thick. When the sea retreated these layers had become sedimentary limestone, now readily apparent throughout the entire region. Repeated pressure sometimes caused cracks resulting in great slabs of tilted rock as can be seen around Entrevaux and Puget-Theniers. Over time erosion by rain and streams has softened the mountainous outlines.

Of the many gorges in southeastern France – the Vésubie, Tinée, Daluis, Verdon, Cians and Var – all stretch some of the way from the Alps to the Mediterranean. In the dry summer it always seems amazing that each trickle of water could carve a deep gorge, yet the winter rains and the spring snowmelt generate fast-flowing rivers. The gorges vary: some are wide, others narrow, some cut into barren limestone while others have fertile soils carrying dense forests and some, like the Cians Gorge, cut through dark red schist. The Vésubie Gorge is deeper and steeper than most.

ROAD THROUGH VESUBIE GORGE

Visiting some of the Vésubie attractions in a single day is possible but that would make it difficult to trace the many side roads that enrich the region. Steep sinuous roads lead to villages, such as Utelle, that were of vital importance to trade during the Middle Ages. The trade routes have long disappeared but the villages remain, preserved almost in their entirety. To the east and north the high altitudes of the Mercantour ranges have generated tributary streams each carving dramatic yet different scenery: the lush waterfalls of the Boréon, the dry Gordolasque and the historically fascinating *Vallon de Madone de Fenestre.*

Further north the mountains close in, effectively creating a land-locked basin from which only a few rough tracks pass through the Mercantour. Rather than back-tracking on the D2565 it is more rewarding to cross the divide at St Dalmas-de-Valdeblore and return through the Valley of the Tinée.

—◦◦◦—

While many kinds of conifer trees flourish at high altitudes it is the larch, the world's only deciduous conifer, that is widespread in the Vésubie, winning the name of *le Roi des Alpes*, the king of the Alps. October sees the dark green needles change to luminous yellow, and in March new pale green foliage appears. In favorable conditions the trees can grow to 20 meters high and live as long as 500 years. Larch timber is tough and durable providing, for example, the piles on which Venice was built. It is still used for boat building and sturdy furniture. The larch often grows in barren soils but its fallen needles enrich the soil and its widely spaced foliage allows a bright and airy forest, encouraging substantial undergrowth, Some of the finest stands are between La Bollène-Vésubie and the *Col de Turini* close to Mercantour National Park. This mountain pass provides the only link between the D2565 on the valley floor and the tortuous D2566 leading to Sospel and the Mediterranean. The huge expanse of forest includes not only the larch but pine, maple, spruce and chestnut trees as well, surprisingly close to the sea as these trees normally thrive in cooler climates.

The strategic location of the *Col de Turini* and the Authion Massif abutting the Italian border has generated many conflicts. In fact the ruined infrastructure of wars – fortifications, barracks and monuments – can all be seen along the 18 kilometer scenic drive known as the *Circuit de l'Authion*. It was here in 1793 that the revolutionary army successfully fought the County of Nice, then part of Savoy. More recently another battle was an especially bitter affair. Following the landings near St Tropez in August 1944, Allied troops quickly liberated Nice. The Germans retreated and consolidated their resources in a defensive position around Authion where they built elaborate fortifications and it was not until April 1945 that Allied forces were victorious.

Sporadic warfare has been a characteristic of these lonely valleys. While the major battles were fought around Authion, the turbulent conditions following the Revolution gave rise to bitter localised conflicts elsewhere. A well-documented clash between loyalist and Revolutionary troops occurred in 1793 near the hamlet of Duranus high above the river, with the loyalists winning. A roadside marker at the northern end of the village, *Belvedere du Saut des Francais* indicates where defeated republican soldiers were forced to jump over the 1,000 meter cliff crying 'Leap for the republic'. The site is a frightening reminder of the horrors of that French Revolution.

―◦∕∕∕◦―

As well as larch forests and monuments to war the Vésubie Valley is widely known for its sanctuaries to the Madonna that have drawn thousands of pilgrims over many centuries. Two are particularly attractive: one close to Utelle and the other to St-Martin-Vésubie. Each of these villages has retained substantial vestiges of early prosperity and

UTELLE: CHURCH OF ST. VERAN

a distinctive character that, in addition to their religious function, make them attractive places to visit.

The road to Utelle branches off the D2565 at St-Jean-la-Rivière and climbs steeply via numerous *lacets* to a height of 800 meters. An ancient settlement, legend has it that Utelle's inhabitants were able to prevent Julius Caesar and his troops from travelling up the valley to conquer Gaul. A stone inscription tells us that Ruffinius of the Eighth Legion was there; yet even before the Romans, in the first century AD a sacred shrine existed in the area.

During the Middle Ages the salt trade generated considerable wealth; sufficient to fund the construction of splendid religious buildings. Two of these remain: the eleventh century Church of Saint Véran and its neighbouring Chapel of the White Penitents. Both have finely carved doors and richly adorned interiors in Baroque style.

Some eight kilometers beyond Utelle is the *Sanctuaire Notre-Dame* that looks over a panorama extending to the Mediterranean. An old building, the chapel reflects its humble beginning. According to legend it was founded in 850AD by Spanish sailors in gratitude for the Madonna's protection during a wild storm at sea. Rebuilt in 1806 after destruction during the Revolution, its simple massive structure comes to life in August each year when pilgrims carry a statue of the Madonna from the Church of Saint Véran for five kilometers to the lonely chapel on the hilltop. In early September it is carried back again.

SANCTUARY OF NOTRE DAME

Near the head of the Vésubie Valley and encircled by forest and mountain summits stands the town of St-Martin-Vésubie. Records show that from 250AD it was held by the Benedictines, the Romans, the Saracens and the Knights Templar. Clearly, ramparts were needed and one of the gates, the Porte-Sainte-Anne, has survived. Important buildings including the mansion of the wealthy Gubernaci family and an eleventh century Romanesque church were strung out along the Rue de Docteur-Canoli, which retains its fast-flowing little stream running down the middle. An important trading center in the Middle Ages, the town later became a popular spa resort and now its proximity to the Mercantour National Park attracts walkers and mountain climbers. In summer the hotels of St-Martin are busy; we stayed at the moderately priced *La Chataigneraie*, enjoying its fine views and simple meals.

For most of the year the seventeenth century Parish Church in St-Martin houses a great treasure: a richly clothed wooden figure of the

MADONE DE FENESTRE

Madone de Fenestre from the twelfth century. In summer each year the Madonna is carried by pilgrims for 12 kilometers along the *Vallon de la Fenestre* to a chapel high in the mountains not far from the Italian border. The term, '*de la Fenestre*' applies to a natural rock formation that resembles a window, clearly visible from the tiny chapel. Although destroyed a number of times, there remains a warm ambience about the chapel and sitting here one feels surrounded by history; there is, for instance, a list of *commandeurs de fenestre*, beginning in 1287. It can be a wonderfully calming experience.

In more recent times, the tolerant community of St-Martin played an important role in helping Jewish people avoid Nazi concentration camps. During the early years of the Second World War the area was administered by Italians who, in contrast to the Nazis, were sympathetic to the Jewish cause. Warned that German administrators were about to take over and believing United States forces would soon invade the Italian peninsula, the Jewish group of around 1,500 people decided to trek east across the mountains to the Piedmont plain in Italy. Those who decided not to go were soon rounded up and sent to Auschwitz. Unfortunately for the majority who decided to go, it was winter and their rough route skirted the *Madone de Fenestre* by way of a particularly difficult pass. Many children and the elderly died from exposure to the cold. Some survived and reached Italy and after the war a few migrated to Australia and Canada.

On the western side of the valley, perched on a rocky spur, is the handsome village of Venanson with striking views of St-Martin and the mountains of Mercantour. Its most precious jewel is the little *Chapelle St-Sebastien* in the central square. Again, the chapel's plain exterior hides an extremely rich interior: superb fifteenth century frescoes illustrating the life of the saint by Jean Baleison of the Nice school of painting.

It is easy to take a contrasting return journey to the coast. Head westward to the prosperous ski resort of St Dalmas-de-Valdeblore at 1,300 meters above sea level, with its fine early Romanesque church. It is usually locked but a woman from the village will come and open it. Here is the entry to the upper Tinée Valley, far gentler than the Vesubie and famous for its spectacular hilltop villages including Roubion, Roure, Marie, Clans and La Tour and their small painted chapels.

Roubion and Roure, both now almost deserted, are difficult to get to but the effort is rewarding. The walls and ceiling of the Chapel of St Sebastien at Roubion are entirely covered with well-preserved frescoes in striking colors. St Sebastien was believed to provide protection from the plague so the chapel in nearby Roure with some quite bizarre paintings is also dedicated to him..

Of the larger villages south of Valdeblore, Marie is probably the most isolated with the highest altitude and certainly the most difficult access road. Very old, it remains essentially a farming village retaining its fine grove of olive trees. The tall buildings and narrow streets, built from the same stone, cluster together on the side of the valley. The need for security was obviously the primary reason for the location of these villages, but a reliable underground water supply was also essential. In Marie in the early summer of 2005 there were many fountains in use and water was running down the main street but the Mayor had signs everywhere warning of possible water shortages later in the summer. Marie has a small hotel with five rooms but, as usual in these villages, it is the church that dominates everyday life. Each September during the *Fête de la Vièrge Marie* the large, heavy statue of the Virgin is taken out of the church and carried through the streets in colorful procession, as has occurred for hundreds of years.

The villages along the Tinée are similar in the way they perch high above the river but, as is so common in rural France, they have always been isolated from each other. No two are the same. Clans, more prosperous than most, has quite a majestic seventeenth century church that sits proudly in one of the numerous squares in the village. About 500 meters below the town the insignificant looking and somewhat derelict *Chapelle Saint Antoine* is in fact unique. Inside, its walls and ceilings are completely covered with well-preserved frescoes by the fourteenth century artist, André de Cella. The simplicity of design and harmonious colors of these 500 year old frescoes in such a modest

CLANS: CHAPELLE SAINT ANTOINE

LA TOUR: CHAPEL OF THE WHITE PENITENTS

building are surprising. The chapel also marks the beginning of a long walking path across an old Roman bridge to Rousillon.

Until quite recently the only connection between Utelle on the Vésubie and La Tour on the Tinée was by way of a tortuous track across the steep mountain ridge between the valleys. La Tour itself focuses on a large open square with an ancient Gothic church. Several buildings are decorated in the *trompe l'oeil* style (a method of painting that creates the illusion of three dimensional space). The tiny Chapel of the White Penitents has walls and ceilings decorated with scenes of the Passion in surprisingly vivid colors considering their 1491 origin. Outside the colors are faded but still beautiful. Most chapels and churches in the perched villages are now locked but asking around or visiting the council office usually produces someone with a key.

It is an easy drive to the south through the serene lower valley of the Tinée until its junction with the Var River. From here the N202 delivers you to Nice in a very short time.

THE HIGH COUNTRY

Chapter Nine

The High Country

When the Romans came to southeastern France they called it Alpa Maritima, a name that has survived to this day. Here the mountains really do come down to the sea; within a short 100 kilometers to the north they rise to over 3,000 meters. Largely unoccupied and with no major towns they form a clear break with the continuous urban development along the coast.

Sliced deeply by short but rapidly flowing north-south rivers, these mountains are difficult to penetrate and, until the early twentieth century, were virtually unknown. Even when roads were eventually built they snaked along the valley floors and east-west links across the mountain ridges were avoided. For centuries tiny communities, though physically close, existed in isolation from each other. Although accentuated here by the ruggedness of the mountains this story is repeated all over rural France: historians now claim that little more than 100 years ago the country was essentially a mosaic of diverse and isolated *pays* each with its own dialect and traditions, and that French was a foreign language to the majority of people.

As well as its wild landscapes and vast empty spaces this mountainous land – *the Haut Pays* - extending from the coast to peaks over 3,000 meters and then down to the gentle Ubaye Valley is home to a large number of solitary villages. Tough rather than beautiful, their dramatic locations on summits or precipitous hillsides immediately attract attention; some have preserved their customs, dialect and religious art and, although access roads can be tricky, a visit is usually memorable. One or two larger towns such as Guillaumes survive as market centers for sheep raising, the most successful activity in this austere environment.

Excellent roads now blaze up the Var Valley opening the mountains to skiers, car-rally drivers and ordinary visitors who like to take their time. The roads are steep, closed by snow for much of the year and often under repair in summer. They cross the high ridges at only three well-defined cols. Given the long periods of warfare between Provence and Savoy it is not surprising to find relics of war along these high roads.

Ranking among the world's great mountain roads, the *Route des*

FIRST CARS ON ROUTE DES GRANDES ALPES

Grandes Alpes extends some 700 kilometers from Menton on the Mediterranean to Thonon-les-Bains on Lake Geneva. Commenced early in the twentieth century, a time of innovation in the automobile industry, it reflected growing interest among the more affluent residents on the Riviera in exploring the high country to the north. Initiated in 1909 by the Touring Club of France, the project took about 30 years to complete; not so long given the nature of the terrain and the number of government agencies that had to be co-ordinated.

Opened in stages, the crossing of each of the sixteen cols on the way to Geneva was a time for celebration. The pass at Vars, for example, was crossed for the first time on July 1, 1911 by a prominent bus company which carried over 1,000 happy travelers. By 1933 the number of travelers had increased to 255,000 a year. Because of its north-south axis the *Route des Grandes Alpes* cuts across a variety of stunning landscapes: glaciers, sharp ridges and peaks, abrupt rock faces, mountain pastures and larch forests. Villages, churches and forts add to the diversity.

The first section of the *Route* leaves Menton and goes directly north over a very winding stretch to Sospel, through some of the best larch forests to be seen anywhere, and over the *Col de Turini* to St-Martin at the head of the Vésubie Valley. A more direct alternative is to take the N202 from Nice along the Var and then into the Tinée Valley. From here the *Route* diverges into three narrow mountain roads, each leading to Barcelonnette, the northernmost town of Provence. Roughly parallel to each other, they provide different ways of crossing the French Alps at the three famous passes: the *Col de la Bonette*, the *Col d'Allos* and the *Col de la Cayolle*, each usually open from early June to mid-October.

Although Bonette is the highest pass, the D2205 is easy driving and the views on the southern side can be magnificent. Valley shelves are farmed in summer to a surprisingly high altitude and the large number of shepherd huts scattered over the mountain sides show that transhumance of sheep and goats is still practised here. A detour to the small village of Auron at 5000 feet, now a well-known ski resort, allows a visit to the *Chapel St Erige* with its rich larch woodwork and magnificent decoration. The remains of two military encampments, one at the top of the pass and a larger one to the south, each occupied by mountain soldiers until the end of the second world war are indicative, again, of the French concern with defense. The *Col de la Bonette*, well above the tree-line is mostly covered by cloud; there are no walking trails here and the bleak landscape with its incredible silence encourages one to hurry down to Jausiers and Barcelonnette in the Ubaye Valley.

A more adventurous route, the D908, passes through the particularly wild country of the upper Verdon Valley where, just north of Colmars, Vauban built one of his most impressive forts. This route over the Alps at *Col d'Allos* is something of a 'white-knuckle' drive as the narrow road literally clings to the precipitous valley sides for long distances but the area is a popular ski resort and in summer a hub for hiking. One of the most popular side trips is to the spectacular *Lac d'Allos*, a drive of about 14 kilometers, then a one-hour walk. Completely unpolluted and surrounded by barren mountains, this is one of the finest glacial lakes to be found anywhere. The third road, the D902, crosses the mountains at *Col de la Cayolle* and leads to the old market town of Guillaumes and two impressive gorges, the *Daluis* and the *Cians*, each cut by tributaries of the Var River.

The town of Barcelonnette is squeezed into the narrow Ubaye glacial valley and enclosed on three sides by towering peaks. It experiences heavy snowfalls and for much of its history has been cut off from other parts of the country; only quite recently has it been connected by road to the Durance Valley. With a mere 3,500 people it is an unusual Provencal town with a fascinating history.

BARCELONNETTE

Originating in the thirteenth century, the name comes from the Counts of Barcelona who had moved up the natural pathway from Spain into the Ubaye Valley and controlled the entire territory until it was captured by the Dukes of Savoy. It differs from most Provencal towns in the grid-like form of the narrow, straight streets intersecting at right angles and focussing on a huge central square, *Place Manuel*, with its white clock-tower commemorating the French Revolution of 1848. On the wall of this tower there is a fine example of a *cadran solaire* (sun dial), a feature of many public buildings in *Haute Provence*, they are a kind of homage to the sun, almost like elaborate frescoes. Most were created by travelling artists from the Piedmont in the eighteenth and nineteenth centuries.

The real story of Barcelonnette, however, began in 1805 when two local businessmen, Jacques and Marc-Antoine Arnaud, decided to escape the grinding poverty brought about by almost constant warfare and to try their luck elsewhere. The brothers, whose names are recorded on the wall of the main church, saw an opportunity in Mexico which at that time was experiencing some turbulence in the formation of a republic. Opened in the heart of Mexico City, their craft and textile shop became so profitable that it started a kind of 'gold rush' from Barcelonnette, and the neighbouring town, Jausiers. By 1900 there were 5,000 families from the Barcelonnette region registered with the French Embassy in Mexico and about 500 fabric and novelty stores all over Mexico owned by the French. The migration continued right up until 1950 and now there is a community estimated at 50,000 Barcelonnettes in Mexico City. Not all were successful and many emigrants died in poverty in their adopted land.

As is so often the case, many who prospered returned to their homeland to build ostentatious houses, bringing a Mexican influence that pervades Barcelonnette in many ways, especially in food and clothing. One of the better inexpensive hotels, and a good base from which to explore the valley (and Le Queyras), the *Hôtel Azteca*, has something Mexican in each room. The strong relationship endures as shown by the long list on the church wall of French living in Mexico who returned, along with many Mexican citizens to fight in the French army in both world wars.

Given the history of the Ubaye Valley, being at different times part of Barcelona, France and Savoy, as well as its close proximity to Italy, the valley has its share of fortresses, none though designed by Vauban.

Just to the east of Barcelonnette three large forts, all in good repair, stand guard. The best known is the *Fort de Tournoux*, clinging to the valley side 2,300 meters above the river; completed in 1863 it is a most impressive piece of military engineering. The *Fort de Roche-la-Croix* and the *Fort de St-Ours-Haut*, of much more recent origin, were built as southern extensions of the Maginot Line, the ambitious French system of forts which failed dismally in the Second World War. In the Alps heavy fighting between French and Italian troops continued around these forts right up until 1945.

⚍☙☙⚎

Deceptively ordinary in appearance, the old market-town of Guillaumes is rich in history. It remained part of Provence from its establishment in the tenth century until ceded to Savoy by Louis XV in 1760. During this time religious wars devastated the countryside as demonstrated by the ruined castle, the *Château de la Reine Jeanne* that broods over the town from a nearby hilltop. The origins of this ruin lay in the Vaudois sect founded by a Lyonnais preacher in the twelfth century. Like the better-known Cathars, the Vaudois strongly opposed what they saw as the extravagance of the Catholic Church and advocated the removal of all religious liturgy. When forced out of Lyon the sect colonised isolated alpine valleys, and the castle at Guillaumes probably dates from this time. In the mid-fifteenth century, as part of the continuing persecution of Protestants, the castle was destroyed by supporters of *La Reine Jeanne*. Later, a smaller citadel was built on the same site.

Although only 100 kilometers from the coast and connected by a good road, Guillaumes still feels like a small isolated mountain town. For many centuries the only link to Nice was a mule trail; nevertheless it has been a hub of commerce at the intersection of routes connecting farming villages in the Var Valley as far north as the *Col de la Cayolle* and in the mountains to the east as far as St Sauveur. This is still the case and its markets, fairs and festivals retain features of medieval mountain life.

A market day in Guillaumes is quite an occasion. Not only do the participants take over the entire town but the event is associated with great festivity; cafes and bars are as busy as the market itself. There is a regular monthly fair, usually on a Saturday, that sells almost everything,

GUILLAUMES: FOIRE AUX TARDONS

including preserved meat and cheeses, plants and flowers, books, new wine and livestock. As well, two major events attract visitors from all over the southeast. The *Foire aux Tardons* on 16 September each year is a market for new lambs from surrounding mountain valleys. The *Grande Foire d'Eté* on 16 August sells an even wider range of goods and involves a pageant and pilgrimage to the sixteenth century church, *Notre Dame de Buyei*, just outside the town: this *Fête de l'Assomption*, when men parade in military uniform outside the church, celebrates those few villagers who made it back from Napoleonic wars.

South of Guillaumes are two of the most beautiful gorges in the Alps running almost parallel to each other: the *Gorges du Cians* accessed by the D28 and the *Gorges de Daluis* by the D2202. The surprising depth of the narrow gorges is explained by the torrents coming from the heavy snow-melt each year which expose an unusually wide range of different colored rock strata, the dominant one being a deep red schist. Striking in the Fall, the amazing burst of colors appears as a celebration of the end of a long hard summer. The red, yellow and green of the trees against the colored rock is something special.

Beuil, now a modern ski resort at the northern tip of the *Gorges du Cians* was once far more important. In Roman times it was Caesar's fortress controlling the movement of troops along the Var and Tinée Valleys in his struggle against the Gauls. Later, in that long period of discord between France and Savoy, being right on the frontier Beuil was of strategic significance to both sides. Along with the farming communities nearby it was controlled for many years by the Grimaldis, one of the ambitious families of *seigneurs* who assumed great authority over these mountain valleys, always at arm's length from the king.

Apart from Guillaumes and a few modern ski resorts like Beuil and Valberg, settlements are few in these mountains. Of those remaining, the small village of Peone is typical: extremely isolated, hidden among a cluster of curious pinnacle, needle-shaped limestone rocks. More obvious are the tiny chapels that punctuate the banks of the *Haut-Var* and have survived the floods, avalanches and rock falls that regularly occur here. As with other chapels in the Tinée Valley, many are superbly decorated, like the Renaissance *Chapelle de St-Sebastien* near Entraunes just north of Guillaumes. Some interesting small towns dot the mid-section of the Var when the valley widens out and the gradient becomes less steep. The attractive village of Touet-sur-Var, for example, at the dramatic southern entry to the *Gorges du Cians* looks down from its cliff-face over the busy N202. And nearby is where Vauban fortified the old perched village of Entrevaux.

Puget-Theniers, a little further down the valley, is an open and welcoming place. It is an important station for the famous *Train des Pignes*, named after the old steam trains connecting Nice with Digne that used pine-cones instead of coal. In summer the diesel engine is replaced by one of the originals at Puget and is very popular with tourists. These little train lines, the *Chemins de Fer de Provence*, are not part of the SNCF system and have a different terminus in Nice.

PUGET: TRAIN DES PIGNES

Unusual for a French village, Puget has a clearly designated old Jewish quarter in the streets that rise steeply up the valley side. The iconic feature, however, is Aristide Malliol's sculpture of a woman with her hands tied behind her back, called *L'Action Enchaînée* in memory of August Blanque, a local hero. Blanque was a revolutionary who participated in numerous nineteenth century popular movements culminating in the Paris Commune of 1871. For his contributions he spent about 40 years in gaol but is rewarded by the inscription on the statue that recognizes 'his fidelity to the cause of workers' emancipation'.

The country immediately to the north of Puget, the *Pays de la Roudoule*, is very rugged and the gorge cut by a small stream has exposed unusual red and black rock formations in an interesting old copper mining area. A short excursion on the D16 following the gorge toward St-Leger passes through this landscape and leads also to a fine Roman bridge at *Pont de St-Leger*. There are actually three bridges here: a modern one, a nineteenth century one underneath and the old Roman bridge, much smaller and lower in the gorge, about a hundred meters downstream.

—◦◊◦—

The perched villages on the plateau immediately south of the high mountains are small, old and solitary. The plateau itself, extending across the pre-Alps from N85 to the Esteron Valley and Vence is a grim and desolate area with deeply-cut *clues* that, together with the low rainfall make farming difficult. For the most part the villages here reflect these conditions and over a long time have become depopulated, even fallen into decay. Some, though, are quite prosperous and actually booming because of gentrification brought about by their proximity to large coastal towns.

Gréolières is one of the oldest villages in this plateau area and looks directly at the feudal chateau in Cipières which, in turn, looks directly at Bezaudan and the tiny village of Courmes perched on the side of the Loup River. Gréolières retains its medieval form and, although commuters to the coast have moved in, giving the place a somewhat sophisticated air, the renovations have not destroyed the original character of the buildings.

A picturesque route across the arid plateau leads south on D17 and D27 from Puget to Roquestron and numerous hilltop villages all originally controlled by the Grimaldi family. Roquestron itself is divided into two reflecting its border location until 1860 although few differences are immediately apparent; Roquesteron-Grasse with its Roman church perched on the right bank of the Esteron River is the original village. On the left bank, Roquesteron-Puget is more modern. The old customs house, important when the frontier separated the two parts, can still be seen on the *Pont de France* the bridge across the river. Old ways of doing things live on and even today the two sections of the one small village have separate *Mairies*.

A little further along the northern side of the Esteron, the ancient village of Pierrefeu is perched high above the river, some four kilometers up a steep slope from the D27. The road passes through some fine olive and vine country to one of the earliest and best known Roman signalling points. The village resembles Saorge in the Roya Valley with its streets, steps, buildings and roofs built from local stone, so that it forms an organic whole with the mountain side.

On the side of the Esteron opposite Pierrefeu, Bouyon is a substantial and lively village looking directly over the junction of the Var and Esteron toward the Alps. Built on two levels it has a communal *boulangerie*, a reminder of its long history, a modern hotel and an *épicerie* - clear indicators of current prosperity. It too was a Roman stronghold and a part of the Grimaldi fiefdom but unlike some frontier towns, since

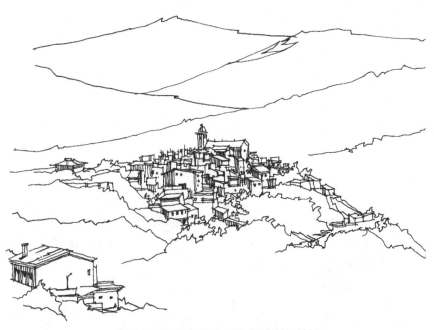

THE PERCHED VILLAGE OF BOUYON

1483 it has remained in French territory. The centerpiece of this village is not a chateau but a large church with a very plain interior except for a fine Louis Brea altarpiece. Bouyon is famous for its procession of the snails, an ancient traditional Christian event, in which thousands of snail shells are filled with oil and lit at night, apparently a spectacular sight; it is a prayer for a good olive harvest.

CÔTES DE PROVENCE WINE AREA

Chapter 10

Rosé : The Wine of The South

Vines have been grown in the south of France for well over 2,000 years making it one of the oldest wine-making areas in the world. The syrah or shiraz grape, originally from Persia, was introduced along the coast near Marseilles by the ancient Greeks and taken further inland by the Roman legions. It produced a very pale red wine, later to be known as rosé. For almost 500 years the grape was confined to Provence - it did not appear on the hillsides of Burgundy, for example, until 310 AD – and was grown then, as now, predominantly on small landholdings. In fact the productivity of the vine made it possible for small independent farmers to live off tiny plots in isolated regions, one reason why an unchanging peasant economy survived for a much longer period in France than elsewhere in Europe.

Inevitably, over this long period the wines produced and the cuisine that developed with them have become integral and distinctive parts of the history and way of life of the south. Most of the wines come from hundreds of vineyards that comprise the *Côtes de Provence* wine region, extending from Draguignan just west of Grasse, to St Tropez on the coast and Aix on the Rhone. Of the huge quantity produced, 80% is rosé, a wine of almost luminous pale red color, very light, fresh with a high alcohol content, dry and always unpretentious. Sometimes scorned as 'eminently unserious' by wine experts it is nevertheless consumed with much pleasure by locals and visitors especially during the hot summers. Drunk in the first year after harvest – vintages mean very little – a chilled bottle of good rosé is something to remember whether it be consumed under the sun at lunch in a village square, or at an evening meal *en plein aire* on a terrace overlooking the Mediterranean when there is nothing ugly to be seen, nothing disagreeable and when the mussels taste of the wine dark sea.

A wine with more pretension than a rosé is simply overwhelmed by the strongly flavored foods of the south, even the most common ones including: pissaladière, a kind of pizza topped with garlic, olives, onions and anchovies; salade nicôise with its hard boiled eggs, garlic, mesclun, olives and tuna or the soupe au pistou, a delicious vegetable soup flavored with pistou, a variant of Italian pesto. And rosé goes particularly well with fish, especially in the evenings in the restaurants that line either side of the Cours Saleya in old Nice or in the more modest eating places in Grasse's Place aux Aires.

The *Côtes de Provence* area is the largest officially designated wine region in France. Until the 1930s a lot of wine was blended, fraudulently labeled and marketed illegally. The government response was to designate certain geographical areas for wine production and to strictly regulate almost every factor that goes into wine making in those areas including the types of grapes, use of fertiliser, irrigation, blending, pruning methods and the maximum harvest per hectare. Determining the boundaries was supervised by the *Appellation d'Origine Controlée* (literally the 'controlled name of origin'), an agency of the French Ministry of Agriculture and only vineyards that are located within the designated area may use that place name. This means French wines are identified on the label by where they were produced rather than by the grapes from which they are made, the common method in many other parts of the world.

But only about 25% of French wine usually considered the best and certainly the most expensive, comes from AOC regions. There are three other classes of wine, many of excellent quality and in some years considered superior to the AOC wines. In order of descending quality and price they are: *Vins Délimité de Qualité Supérieure* (VDQS), wines that come from a specific place but outside the AOC areas, *Vin de Pays*, which really means local wines and *Vin de Table* or *vin ordinaire*, often sold in liter bottles and small casks in supermarkets. Wines in all four categories are readily accessible in supermarkets, autoroute stops, specialist wine shops and from the *cave* or cellar door.

———⁓———

There is much to be said for visiting the cellars of the vineyards: it allows tasting and buying (*dégustation et vente*), meeting those associated with the winery, entry to some excellent buildings and, above all, an opportunity to see a unique wine-producing countryside with dozens of fine old villages. The *Côtes de Provence* region is quite compact and the vineyards clearly identified on the roadside and accessible via a network of narrow roads. The wineries, known as chateaux or domaines are familiar because their names are proudly displayed on their bottles everywhere, reflecting the French belief that every chateau, no matter how small, produces wine that strictly speaking cannot be duplicated elsewhere – something to check out on a *dégustation* visit. The French argue there are variations over even very small distances in the *terroir*, which means the combined influence of soil, sun, rainfall, viticulture and the slope of the land. Soil is the most important, with alluvial soil always avoided.

Of the large number of chateaux only 28 have been awarded *Crus Classé* status, meaning they are recognized for producing consistently good quality wines. Their rosé comes from the skins of several grapes including grenache, shiraz, cinsault and mourvèdre, and calls for considerable wine-making skills as the juice can only be kept in contact with the skins for a few hours and needs constant checking for color, crispness and delicacy. At least three *Crus Classé* chateaux are worth a serious visit: Chateau Minuty on the coast near St Tropez, Roubine near Lorgues and, especially, Ste-Roseline with its lovely old chateau and cellar near Les Arcs. But, given variations in *terroir*, the seasons and changes in wine-makers the unsuspecting visitor can come across some surprisingly attractive wines from little known vineyards outside the AOC boundary. Some personal favorites are: Chateau Thuerry at Villecroze, Domaine Sainte Jean also at Villecroze, Chateau de Rouet near Draguignan and St André de Figuière near Hyères.

Before taking off on a one or two day tour of the *Côtes de Provence* it is important to understand that in appearance it has little in common with France's smaller and perhaps better known wine regions. The buildings and villages reflect its long history. Do not expect anything like the spectacular slopes of Burgundy or the lush green scenery around the Loire or Bordeaux. Rather, here one confronts the hard face of Provence: flat dry land, baked hard by the fierce summer sun, acidic soils and a vegetation of stunted shrubs and bushes of the *garrigues*, interspersed with holm oaks. Except for the land near St Tropez it is swept by the dreaded mistral. There remains however a barren austere beauty to much of this wine country; and some patches of brilliance like where the red rocks of the Esterel and Massif des Maures - the early home of the Saracens - contrast sharply with the pale limestone soil. Many vineyards are discreetly located off the roads in the midst of the scrub-like vegetation where their verdant appearance comes as something of a surprise. They are never irrigated, winters are cold, rainfall low and while the intense heat of early summer gives the wines their distinctive flavor it can also bring devastating bush fires. The early summer of 2003, for example, saw many vineyards in the central Var *Département*, immediately west of Grasse, swept by fires but the wine produced that year is considered to be among the best ever.

The east-west A8 autoroute effectively divides the region into two parts. The southern part, stretching from the A8 to Fréjus, St Tropez and Hyères on the Mediterranean, is dominated by the Massif des Maures and the Massif de l'Esterel, two expanses of unused land, so common in rural France, and the grapes are confined to a narrow coastal strip. There are some very good vineyards here, especially near the attractive towns of St Tropez and Cogolin but, for most of the year, visiting them can be a nightmare: only one two-lane road runs from the A8 to St Tropez and it is clogged with tourist traffic much of the time.

It is far better to concentrate on the areas to the north of the A8, including the Valley of the Argens, a very old wine area, usually referred to by locals simply as 'the Var'. A useful starting point for a visit is the *Maison des Vins* on Route Nationale 7 immediately before the entry to Les Arcs (a little difficult to locate but take the Draguignan-St Tropez exit from the A8). This is the largest cooperative sales center and, as well as its cellar of over 400 locally-produced wines, it displays maps, photographs and descriptions of localities that are helpful in arranging visits. And you can taste and stock up from their cellar.

From here there are numerous signposted wine routes, but experience suggests it is best to find one's own way around: there is a dense network of roads with little traffic connecting the small villages and all the main vineyards. This may necessitate some back-tracking as the chateaux are not always easy to see, often located some kilometers off the road and hidden in stunted scrub. We recommend a clockwise route starting from Les Arcs and moving around to Draguignan and Nice.

Les Arcs itself is worth exploring, especially the Romanesque *Chapelle Sainte-Roseline*, four kilometers east on D91. The chapel and cloisters are all that remain of the original Abbey of *La Celle Roubard* founded in 1038. The interior of the chapel, open only in the afternoons, houses the remains of Ste. Roseline. On the initiative of a benefactor,

CHATEAU SAINTE-ROSELINE

Marguerite Maeght, some outstanding modern works of art have been installed, including a Chagall mosaic and a bronze lectern by Diego Giacometti. Next door is one of the *Cru Classé* vineyards of the *Côtes de Provence*, Chateau Sainte-Roseline, whose prestige is reflected in the fine chateau building, its sales room and the price of the wines. The owners will organize tours of the chateau and the vineyard.

Vidauban, a few kilometers to the west on the flat plain of the sluggish Argens River, is one of the oldest villages of the central Var. Nearby is the Chateau d'Astros, well-known for producing a surprisingly good quality, flinty *vin de pays*, the least-expensive type of wine. At le Thoronet is the oldest of the three existing Cistercian abbeys in Provence, others being at Sénanque and Silvacane, the latter in a very good state of repair. Construction work at Thoronet began in 1160 when a group of Cistercian monks came from the Ardèche region after a brief stay at Tourtour and settled here. At its peak it housed about 20 monks but fell into decline and by 1790 was on the verge of complete ruin. Restoration work has been going on irregularly ever since and the church and restored cloisters are now particularly impressive. The Romanesque church has a simple style: its walls are constructed of stones cut so they fit together without mortar and its interior is of the barrel-vault type. Overall a proportional and spatial simplicity gives the old abbey an austere beauty. And the Domaine de l'Abbaye nearby produces a fine rosé, its quality allegedly coming from picking the grapes in the cool at night; it is sold in distinctive blue bottles to protect it from the light.

ABBAYE DE THORONET

The small town of Cotignac is at the foot of a limestone cliff riddled with caves that were used many years ago for the storage of wine; its main street, Cours Gambetta, has shops selling local products including wine of fairly ordinary quality. At this point there is the option of continuing northward to Villecroze and Tourtour with the possibility of visiting the Verdon Gorge or go westwards to Entrecasteaux and Lorgues. Given the short distances, it is advisable to make a round trip: this is the beginning of the *Haut Var* with its cooler temperatures and more attractive hilly, wooded landscapes.

Although quite tranquil at present, some villages had a turbulent past, experiencing attacks by barbarians and, later, by the Saracens. Lorgues' impressive fortifications illustrate the uncertainties of the Middle Ages. Particularly interesting are its still-intact fortified gateways or *portes* built as tunnels that allowed entry at only a few places through the walls to the town center. Today, however, as the southernmost town in *la route de la truffe* its history and indeed its wine are secondary in importance to its black truffles, *le rabasse*, the so-called black gold of the *Haut Var*. A string of villages to the north, including Bargemon, Seillans, Mons and Chateaudouble all reflect the prosperity that goes with black truffles. A truffle market is held in Aups every Thursday during the winter season, climaxing in a huge truffle fair on the fourth Sunday in January.

The old part of Villecroze with strong walls, winding cobbled streets and stairways, stone arches, vaulted lanes and a communal washing area is entirely medieval. The Domaine Sainte Jean de Villecroze, two kilometers to the east on the road to Draguignan, is one of two vineyards in this higher country generally regarded as producing some of the very best wines. St Jean was rescued from a run-down condition by an American buyer who installed modern equipment and introduced new vines, all grown without the use of fertilizers, insecticide or fungicide sprays.

VIGNERON JEAN-LOUIS CROQUET

A little further along the Draguignan road, Chateau Thuerry is of more interest because of the warm welcome that English-speaking visitors receive from the vigneron Jean-Louis Croquet. Chateau Thuerry is typical of the larger estates: it dates back to the twelfth century but the current owners have invested heavily in new cellars, which can be visited, and in new wine-making technology. As with Sainte Jean, they maintain traditional methods of farming involving no fertilizer, and, of course, no irrigation. The Chateau produces rosés, whites, reds and a fine *blanc de blanc champenoise* and, at the time of our visit, had a display of contemporary sculpture in front of the chateau. As well as being an excellent vigneron, M.Croquet is knowledgeable about Californian and Australian wines and is an ardent rugby union fan.

Tourtour, a medieval perched village, nestles in soft, green hills, a more attractive landscape than the scrubby lands just to the south; although very small it is more lively than Villecroze. Narrow lanes converge on the central square where people gather for coffee under some particularly attractive old plane and olive trees. The latter replace two famous elm trees planted in 1683 by Anne d'Autriche, the Queen of France. It is historically a rich town: the Aurelian Way, one of the most important roads in the Roman Empire, linking Rome, Genoa, Nice and Aix-en-Provence, was taken up from the coast at Fréjus through Draguignan, a major military base, through Tourtour and on to Aix. Stretches of the road are still used just east of the town. In 1136 Cistercian monks founded the Abbaye de Floreille, later relocated to Thoronet; the ruins can be seen four kilometers along the road to Ampus, about 500 meters before a Roman bridge still in use.

There are fine views over the Argens Valley and Mont Victoire from the eleventh century church in Tourtour which has a rather lonely location on the edge of the town. Set in particularly attractive countryside, a good place to break a journey and savor some of the local wines is the *Auberge St-Pierre* about four kilometers to the east

TOURTOUR: CENTRAL SQUARE

of Tourtour on the D51. Built on a steeply-sloping hillside farm of 90 hectares the hotel has lovely views over forest and cleared land with lots of grazing animals - a very tranquil spot.

The largest town in the wine region and probably the least visited, Draguignan has suffered from being a military base throughout its entire history. Its original Roman fort was built where the clock tower stands today; from it a defensive wall with three gates and a keep were built. It was important in Napoleon's time; he made it the administrative center of the Var which helps explain why those familiar with the grand boulevards of Paris may recognize some similarities in the street pattern of Draguignan. In the mid nineteenth century when he was *préfet* of the Var, Baron Haussman had something of a trial run here and laid out a number of tree-lined straight boulevards which, although pretty dusty today, continue to be a feature in the center of the town. As the largest military base in France it has interesting war memorials, notably the American War Cemetery containing the graves of 861 Americans from the 7th Army who were killed in Provence following the 1944 Allied landings.

If rosé is the wine of the south, Ricard is the number one spirit (outselling whisky, gin and vodka combined), consumed primarily as an aperitif but also at any time of the day or night. A blend of star anise and licorice, this 45% alcohol drink resembles ouzo, raki and arak, all drunk around the shores of the Mediterranean, but the quality and harmony of Ricard's ingredients give it a unique flavor. Created by the eccentric Paul Ricard in 1932 the process remains the same: the main ingredient, star anise is imported from southern China and licorice which gives the fragrance, from Syria. At Marseilles they are blended with aromatic herbs from Provence into a smooth drink. Traditionally served with five parts water and one part Ricard, the drink *louches* or turns cloudy; apparently sweeter than it actually is, one glass can follow another with treacherous ease.

AUBERGE ST. PIERRE

Ricard should never be drunk on the rocks: it will be very strong, non-refreshing and immediately become scummy. And like rosé it needs sunshine. Ricard is very much a summer drink; just the smallest glass summarises an entire sea and its defining season.

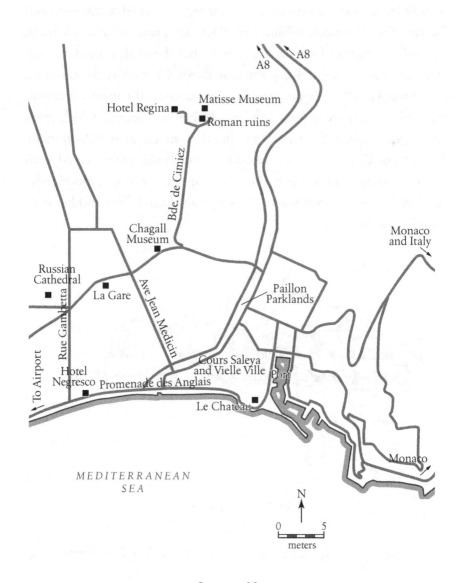

CENTRAL NICE

Chapter Eleven

And Then There is Nice

Living in the foothills of the Alps is a uniquely rewarding experience but occasionally one feels drawn to the urbanity of a big city. It is then we head for Nice – as do many others. After Paris, it is the second most popular French city with tourists, sparkling in brilliant sunshine in both winter and summer. Irrespective of the number of times we return we are caught up in the sheer beauty of the Bay of Angels with its four kilometer, palm lined *Promenade des Anglais* along the sensual curve of the beach. All too soon, though, reality asserts itself. As it has been colonized by tourists the city has lost much of its historic and raffish charm. Instead there is nightmare traffic, the near impossibility of parking a car and hordes of people baking on hard stones at the waterfront. To new arrivals however, Nice is an immediately seductive city. By the time they get off the planes, which always come in across the bay, visitors have had a entrancing glimpse of some of the very best the place has to offer. You can tell they have high expectations as, dressed for action in the sun, they charge through the airport and hurtle toward mainly over-priced hotels, by what could well be one of the most expensive taxi journeys in the world.

There is nothing new about this invasion; indeed, people have been coming here for many centuries by carriages, cars, trains, ships and planes. Archeologists have even found evidence of Stone Age people

NICE IN THE 1950s

living in caves along the coast between Nice and Menton and of Neolithic dwellers - Ligurians and Celts - who came around 2000 BC to grow crops, graze animals and carve on rocks in the Valley of the Marvels. The fourth century BC saw Greeks arrive by way of Marseilles and establish a trading center near the prominent hill (the Chateau) at the eastern end of what is now the *Promenade des Anglais*; from the nearby elevator one can see some of the sparse ruins of this early settlement but also enjoy views of the coast, the old town and the port.

Preoccupied with fighting the Punic Wars and consolidating their hold on the Italian peninsula, it was not until the first century BC that the Romans came to colonise Gaul. Although many individuals played important parts in this territorial thrust, the family of Julius Caesar was most heavily involved. Around 100 BC Caesar's uncle, General Marius, defeated a huge army of northern tribesmen who had pushed south to gain the rich farmland of the Rhone Valley and while he waited for his enemy to appear, in true Roman engineering spirit, Marius organized the construction of canals from the Durance River to the Mediterranean. Julius Caesar himself was given command of Roman Gaul and in 57 BC he led his troops, via the Vésubie Valley, over the Alps to subdue the Gallic tribes. Within a few years he had enlarged Roman Gaul as far as the Rhine River and built networks of roads, bridges and canals; by the time he died the Roman Empire had expanded as far north as the English Channel.

LA TURBIE: THE ALPINE TROPHY

Caesar's great-nephew, Augustus, accomplished even more: grand cities with grand buildings – temples, public baths, amphitheaters and monuments. A good example is the Alpine Trophy, a huge monument at La Turbie, about 15 kilometers east of Nice overlooking Monaco, built to commemorate his victories over rebellious Alpine tribes. Originally 50 meters high with rows of columns and marble statues, despite extensive damage during the Middle Ages, it remains an impressive structure.

The most direct route from Rome to southern Gaul was the Aurelian Way that ran along the section of the Mediterranean coast where mountains slope sharply into the sea. As this highway was gradually extended toward Spain, the old Greek port at Nice was ideally located to prosper as a trading and administrative center supporting a population of around 20,000. In the modern suburb of Cimiez a small section of the old Roman town remains, notable especially for its public baths and small amphitheater for gladiatorial combat.

The most remarkable Roman ruins however, are in western Provence, a drive of a few hours from Nice. At Arles, a town favored by Julius Caesar, the key sites are the huge amphitheater (*Arènes*) from the first century AD and capable of seating around 25, 000 people; a vast underground grain store (*Cryptoporticus*) and a sober, green and shady cemetery (*Les Alyscamps*) with many interesting sarcophagi. Chosen by Augustus as the capital of Gaul, Nimes too has some outstanding buildings: an amphitheater similar to the one at Arles and the *Maison Carrée*, a small yet superb temple that, incredibly, has survived in almost perfect form for 2,000 years. And twenty kilometers from Nimes is the

NIMES: LA MAISON CARRÉE

Pont du Gard, an aqueduct considered to be one of the engineering marvels of the Roman world. From the fifth century AD southeastern France was overrun by barbarian tribes. Most of the great engineering achievements were destroyed or abandoned to the elements but, surprisingly, the commercial function of Nice survived.

—————

During the Middle Ages there was considerable unrest in the southeast. Powerful neighbors, especially Provence and Savoy, fought for control of the region until the fifteenth century when Nice handed itself over to the Duke of Savoy. Increasingly heretical views of the doctrines of the Catholic Church generated dissensions serious enough to lead to wars of religion. The Crusades led to a major expansion in the trade of goods and ideas with the Orient; and Nice prospered as a free port for the salt trade from the Rhone delta through the Roya Valley to Turin.

Around 1500 AD land east of the Var River became part of the Kingdom of Savoy, a firm ally of England, which encouraged a slow trickle of English people desperately seeking solace from their miserable winters to come to Nice; a trickle that over the next 300 years became a torrent. These *hivernants* had quite an impact. They bought up cheap land along the foreshore and hired low-cost Italian labor to build a collection of bizarre architectural follies, including a maharajah's palace, neo-gothic spires and a Moorish fantasy. In the 1820s they financed the construction of what has become the city's dominant visual feature: the *Promenade des Anglais*.

Then came the Russians, especially after a rail link was built between Nice and St Petersburg in 1864. First there were the royals, followed by the writers such as Tolstoy and Chekhov, those connected with the ballet including Stravinsky and Pavlova and painters like Chagall and

Kandinsky; a Russian Orthodox cathedral with classic green-gold onion domes still functions on the Boulevard du Tzarewitch. Many artists were attracted by the brightness of the light, clear air and warmth and their legacy can be seen in a host of local museums: the Matisse and Chagall in Nice, the Renoir at Haut Cagnes, the Léger at Biot, the Annonciade at St Tropez and the Maeght Fondation at St Paul. In the 1920s and 1930s wealthy American swingers discovered the *Côte d'Azur*, led by the tragic Scott and Zelda Fitzgerald, followed by Hemingway, Ford Madox Ford and Edith Wharton. After the war they came in increased numbers from all over: Ali Khan, Rita Hayworth, Somerset Maugham, Jean Cocteau, Daryl Zanuck and Aristotle Onassis. And the list goes on.

This influx of the rich and famous certainly brought high visibility to the *Côte d'Azur* and created an image of affluence, outrageous behavior, fast cars and fast money. A few highly decorated villas remain along the Promenade and some magnificent ones at nearby Cap Ferrat, Villefranche and Monaco. The Hotel Negresco with its pink dome, a fine example of over-the-top *belle époque* architecture, still stands proudly beside the beach.

But Nice is a city of contradictions as shown by the affair of the *Palais de la Méditerranée*, the Nice casino built in 1929 in Art Deco style and described in its early days as probably the most luxurious building the world has ever known. The owner was declared bankrupt in mysterious circumstances in the 1970s and the building was recently demolished. In 1982 Graham Greene, a resident of Antibes, felt compelled to write *J'Accuse: The Dark Side of Nice* which began with a blistering critique of these events: '*Avoid the region of Nice which is the preserve of some of the most criminal organizations in the south of France: they deal in drugs; they have attempted...to take over the casinos in the famous war which left one victim, ... the daughter of the main owner of the Palais de la Méditerranée missing, believed murdered*'.

For its 350,000 permanent residents Nice is a big, rough informal city. A veneer of sophistication, affluence and elegance co-exists with poverty, particularly ugly suburbs, large numbers of unemployed immigrants and a high rate of crime. But the short-term visitor comes only to see the good things and with that in mind the best approach to Nice is to experience the sea front, the old town, the corniches leading to Monaco and the galleries in Cimiez; that is, to virtually ignore the main part of the town.

The Bay of Angels deserves to be seen from on high as, for example, from the fifth floor of the small, double-glazed rooms in the *Hotel Suisse*, one of the more affordable in Nice. The beaches, unfortunately, are for the most part controlled by hotels, each with distinctive umbrellas and chairs, which virtually isolate them from the public. While some hotels import sand, the beaches are mainly covered by large stones that in summer become almost too hot for walking. For anyone not staying at one of the big hotels it is simply very difficult to find a place to swim.

Arguably the best part of Nice is the old town, the *Vieille Ville*, which owes its distinctiveness to an Italian heritage. On the eastern side of the Paillon Parklands which effectively divide Nice into two is the *Cours Saleya*, an extremely attractive urban space with bright market umbrellas, glowing fruit and vegetables and mounds of olives. In the winding medieval streets tiny shops sell antiques, books and hardware but most tempting are the food shops. A *poissonerie* sells six types of oysters, four kinds of mussels, fresh sardines and tiny live crabs. At the many *boulangeries* there are slices of *pissaladière* topped with onions and anchovies also delicious lemon tarts. Slices of socca, a pancake made with chickpea flour and cooked in a wood oven, are a local favorite.

The suburb of Cimiez has two of the very best museums along the Riviera, the Matisse and the Chagall. Henri Matisse lived in Nice

COURS SALEYA

from 1917 to 1954, first in a house on the Cours Saleya and then in the Hotel Regina in Cimiez. The effects of the sea's luminous atmosphere are reflected in his move from sombre, still-life paintings to a virtual explosion of violent color in his Fauve period. From 1930 Matisse focused more on sensual patterns: female bodies, circles of dancers and cut-outs, especially those of rich blue on a white background. The museum is in a beautifully restored seventeenth century Italian villa, the dark external walls of which are decorated with *trompe l'oeil* paintings of windows that really are quite deceiving. The remains of a small medieval garden are in a nearby park which has street names reflecting the long interest in jazz music in this part of the world.

A little further down the hill on Cimiez Boulevard is the Chagall Museum. Of Jewish-Russian background, Marc Chagall spent some years at Vence and this modern airy building contains a substantial collection of his works. The powerful biblical themes in translucent colors glow from stained glass, mosaics, ceramics and tapestries; especially moving is the *Song of Songs* series of paintings.

The Museum of Modern and Contemporary Art is located on the *Promenade des Arts* in the Paillon Parkland. Allegedly linked to the shady activities of Jacques Médicin, it is well worth a visit because of the building itself as well as the contents. Its design echoes the Beauborg in Paris and works displayed are from 1960 onward, with emphasis on local artists such as Yves Klein and Martial Rayasse.

Many of Nice's old villas have either been destroyed or converted into apartments but there are some that give a glimpse of the wealth invested in glamorous lifestyles and fabulous natural settings. A little out of town, St-Jean-Cap Ferrat must rank as one of the most exclusive residential areas in the world and has attracted the likes of Noel Coward, the Windsors and Somerset Maugham. The *Villa Ephrussi de Rothschild* has a museum and gardens open to the public. The pink and white Italianate mansion contains a collection of mosaics, tapestries and furniture as well as works by Renoir, Sisley and Monet; yet it is the

VILLA EPHRUSSI DE ROTHSCHILD GARDENS

143

garden and views that take one's breath away. Early in the twentieth century the Baroness refashioned the landscape by flattening the hilltop to create terraces for gardens of different styles: from Versailles, Florence, Spain, England and Japan. It all represents gardening on a grand scale, undertaken at a time when the natural was scorned and artificial designs were lauded.

This then, was the enchanting face of Nice, a place with which the rich and famous fell in love; even Queen Victoria came under its spell and visited it seven times in what were apparently her happiest years, the last decade of her life. And foreigners came to get away from it all whether it was the northern climate, social restraints or financial problems. Land was cheap and developers flourished, as did gambling and crime; life was easy and lots of money was made.

In a highly centralized country Nice is about as far away from Paris, the capital, as you can get. Perhaps correctly, the locals feel aggrieved by the way their city is neglected, if not scorned by Paris in the spending of public money. It is sometimes argued that the voting habits of the Nicois are more directed against Paris than necessarily supportive of ultra-conservative politics. Those who live there permanently give Nice a genuine identity - tough, affable and informal. On balance they are remarkably tolerant of visitors and in our experience always helpful and friendly – despite our deplorable mangling of their beautiful language.

End Note

The pre-Alps and mountains of the southeastern corner of France are frequently dismissed by travel writers and visitors as little more than a backdrop to the prestigious coastal shoreline, the *Côte d'Azur*. This is understandable as the grey-blue mountains appear forbidding and empty while the coastal strip is immediately attractive and even glamorous. And, although it has problems arising from mass tourism this particular coastline contains little of the detritus that characterizes so many other parts of the Mediterranean today.

But once penetrated, the *arrière pays* and the mountains beyond reveal a fascinating world of astonishing variety: isolated valleys and villages, grandiose and austere scenery, the pathways of great historical figures, all taking us back in time. This is a part of France that a contemporary historian has described as a land where the past did not move seamlessly into the future and 'as a world of ancient tribes and huge vacant spaces.' Diversity is the rule and homogeneity the exception in most of rural France.

Moreover much of France outside Paris remained little known to foreign and even French visitors for many years. Small, self-contained communities-or *pays*-whose universe often extended no further than 20 kilometers retained their secrets well, even including such splendid features as the Canyon of the Verdon and Bronze Age engravings in the Mercantour National Park.

In many respects, then, regional France is an explorer's paradise and the short journeys described in this book were stimulated by an urge to find out more about a part of this hidden area, so close to one of the best known tourist attractions in the world. They uncovered many surprises ranging from the unspoilt purity of the mountains, their gorges, flora and fauna to dozens of medieval villages and tiny picturesque chapels with hidden treasures. The latter were of particular interest; for example the fifteenth century frescoes in the tiny *Notre-Dame-des Fontaines* near La Brigue, in the even smaller Chapelle St-Antoine near Clans and in the *Chapelle des Pénitents-Blancs* at La Tour, the striking colors in the Romanesque *Collegiate Notre-Dame-de-L'Assomption* in Tende and the oddity of *Notre-Dame de Brusc* near Valbonne where, until quite recently, it was believed that the patron saint could bring rain so the worshippers always carried an umbrella when they came to church.

As elsewhere in the Mediterranean there is no escape from history. In fact places whether they be man-made or natural can only be understood in their historical context. Fortunately the Mediterranean environment is supremely evocative and brings place and space together in a unique manner. As the great historian, Fernand Braudel expressed it in his *Memory and the Mediterranean* : 'this is a sea that patiently recreates for us scenes from the past, breathing new life into them, locating them under a sky and in a landscape that we can see with our own eyes, a landscape and sky like those of long ago. A moment's concentration or daydreaming, and that past comes back to life.'